The Naughty Book for Girls

The Naughty Book for Girls

Candice Hill

First published in Great Britain in 2010 by
Michael O'Mara Books Limited
9 Lion Yard
Tremadoc Road
London SW4 7NQ

A CIP catalogue record for this book is available from the British Library.

Papers used by Michael O'Mara Books Limited are natural, recyclable products
made from wood grown in sustainable forests. The manufacturing processes
conform to the environmental regulations of the country of origin.

ISBN: 978-1-84317-380-9

1 2 3 4 5 6 7 8 9 10

www.mombooks.com

Designed and typeset by Joanne Omigie

Front cover image © 2003 Time Tunnel, Inc.

Contents

Acknowledgements   7

Introduction   9

Naughty Girls   11

What's Your Type?   12
Vintage Vamps   24

Daily Doses of Naughtiness   35

Playing at Work   36
The Naughty Guide to Money   44
Minxing the Shops   48
Truth or Dare   52

Let's Get Physical   57

Getting Fit the Naughty Way   58
Dirty Dancing   63
Cheeky Cosmetics   74

Licentious Lingerie 78
Fashion for Passion 85

The Mating Game 91

The Art of Flirting 92
Dating with Attitude 110
Seductive Hints 119
Cooking for Pleasure 121
Somewhere for the Weekend 130

Strictly Bedroom 137

Pillow Talk 138
Erogenous Zones 144
The Pleasure Principle 151
Flights of Fantasy 160

Just for Fun 167

Answers to Questions You Never Dared Ask 168
Fictional Floozies 175
How Naughty are You? 178

Acknowledgements

Naughty girls everywhere have inspired this book, along with the occasional cheeky boy. (You know who you are!) My biggest thanks go to Hannah Knowles, whose brilliant idea this was: first she commissioned me and then she encouraged me every naughty step of the way. She's a natural, intuitive editor. Thanks also go to Joskaude Pakalkaite for her wonderful illustrations, to Joanne Omigie for her fabulous design and to Michael O'Mara's excellent publicist Ana Sampson.

Introduction

When was the first time you were naughty? Did you eat a forbidden biscuit? Hit your baby brother over the head and blame your sister? Hide when your mum was calling you? Stick your tongue out at the neighbours? Even if you can't remember when it was and what you did, the memory of that first deliciously roguish thrill lives on somewhere inside you. This book is about tapping into the side of you that can't resist a little mischief: hey, the naughty step can actually be a great place to be.

Yes, sometimes it's good to be bad. In fact, at times, there's nothing better; especially if you've had one of those days when you've been underestimated, undermined or under the thumb. Unleashing your inner devilry can be very liberating. It's also a lot of fun, whether you're at the shops, at a party, in the boardroom or in the bedroom. Giggling is the essence of top-notch impishness; what's more, it's easy, pleasurable and free. So let go and misbehave: dance yourself dizzy, flirt yourself silly, play pranks and indulge in a little monkey business. Miss Demeanour laughs more than Miss Tweedy Pants any day.

It's time to throw away your ugly underwear, shed your inhibitions, say what you want to say and do what you want to do. Blow a raspberry in the face of convention and follow it up with a sexy pouty kiss. Cook up an erotic storm and nibble it dressed only in your knickers. You too can be the honey to the bees if you learn to be a little bit wicked, with some lessons from naughty girls throughout history who knew the secrets of living life to the full. So enjoy *The Naughty Book for Girls* and revel in some frolics, because every girl deserves to have some saucy fun. Go on, you know you want to!

What's Your Type?

> " When I'm good, I'm very good.
> But when I'm bad I'm better. "
>
> *Mae West*

The naughty girl, that archetypal seductress, is a sensual agent provocateur. Beautiful, independent, charming, clever, witty and dangerous, she entices and provokes saucy deeds and acts of passion.

The most interesting and powerful men of her generation bend to her every whim. With each successful conquest, her mythological status grows. She's a scintillating melting pot of talents and virtues and comes in many different forms …

Sex Kitten

Sex kittens exude a carefree, playful sexuality, hint at moodiness and possess sharp little claws: the 1960s sex symbol Brigitte Bardot was the classic example of this type of minx. Beautiful and pouty, with an air of innocence, she was the pin-up of the decade. One of her lovers said of her: 'I felt a beautiful warmth with Bardot, but found it difficult to discuss things in any depth whatsoever.'

As well as having four husbands and countless conquests to her name, she has starred in forty-eight films, recorded eighty songs, popularized the bikini and the resort of St Tropez, and has had her look and style imitated by countless women, including Kate Moss.

Are you a sex kitten?

♡ Do you live for the moment?

♡ Is self-grooming a form of seduction with you?

♡ Do you purr when you are stroked?

♡ Is life too short for deep conversation?

♡ Do you lash out at the slightest irritation?

If you answered yes to three or more of the questions on page 13, you are a bona fide sex kitten, so get on those Bardot gingham bikinis and playsuits!

Child-Woman

To the child-woman, sex is as natural as eating an ice lolly. Marilyn Monroe was the ultimate combination of sex appeal and innocence. Her effect on men, however, was far from innocent. Her publicist Roy Craft said of her, 'She had such a magnetism that if fifteen men were in a room with her, each man would be convinced he was the one she'd be waiting for after the others left.'

However, a large part Marilyn's allure, like that of any child-woman, was a seeming inability to understand or control the power of her sexuality. Cary Grant, her co-star in *Monkey Business*, recalled that, 'She seemed very shy, and I remember that when the studio workers would whistle at her, it seemed to embarrass her.'

She was, however, a delicious tease. When asked what she wore in bed, she replied, 'Chanel No. 5.' She disliked wearing underwear and reportedly stripped off the moment she got home.

Despite director Billy Wilder's assessment that Marilyn was 'scared and unsure of herself', she starred in several of the biggest box-office hits of the 1950s, married the playwright Arthur Miller and baseball superstar Joe DiMaggio and allegedly had affairs with JFK and his brother Bobby Kennedy. It is this paradox of vulnerability and strength combined that makes the child-woman so intoxicating to men.

Do you qualify as a child-woman?

♡ Are you a naturally sensuous person?

♡ Does every new thing surprise you?

♡ Does underwear feel like a chastity belt?

♡ Are you shy about your sexuality but love to tease?

♡ Do you feel vulnerable, yet powerful, around men?

Did you say yes to at least three of the above? If so, you have the same magnetism as Marilyn. Take a leaf out of her fashion book and wear white – she loved it; it made her look dazzling and innocent at the same time.

Artistic Siren

Artistic sirens are mysterious creative forces, with a rich inner world. They crackle with fiery independence, yet men swarm around them like moths to a blazing fire.

Born in 1907, beautiful Mexican artist Frida Kahlo battled the effects of childhood polio and multiple injuries from a later car crash to create extraordinary art. Most of her paintings were self-portraits, symbolically expressing her pain and sexuality.

She made the first move on famous Mexican painter Diego Rivera and they married in 1929, despite her mother's disapproval. The marriage was tempestuous and both were wildly unfaithful, she with Leon Trotsky and various women, he with her sister Cristina among others. Turbulent relationships and uncontrollable passions such as Frida's are the hallmark of the artistic siren.

Does your creative spirit arouse desire?

♡ Are you bursting with ideas?

♡ Do works of art set your soul on fire?

♡ Are you driven to express yourself, sexually and artistically?

♡ Do your passions run high?

♡ Are men and women seduced by your creativity?

You don't need to count up answers to know if the artistic flame burns inside you, and as for sartorial tips, artists wear whatever the hell they want to.

Pioneering Playgirl

Pioneering seductresses live for adventure and can't stand the chains of domesticity or marriage. They rove the planet looking for excitement and challenge.

Brought up in Kenya, Beryl Markham was a true adventurer. As a teenager, she had a tribal boyfriend who introduced her to the thrilling world of licentious, carefree sex. Her alarmed father married her off at sixteen, but she was repeatedly unfaithful to her husband.

She ran off with a rich aristocrat, but continued to indulge her sexual impulses and had an affair with the Duke of Gloucester, among others. His mother, Queen Mary, was so horrified that she bought Beryl off with £15,000, a fortune in 1929, which virtually set her up for life. She could now take up flying aeroplanes in her beloved Africa. During this time, she apparently had twelve lovers simultaneously, all of whom were reportedly dumbstruck by their erotic experiences with her.

After working as a bush pilot, she decided to fly across the Atlantic. Thirty people had already attempted it and several had died, but when she crash-landed with frozen fuel tanks in Nova Scotia after twenty hours over the sea, she was hailed as the first person to fly solo from Europe to America.

Are you an adventurous lover?

♡ Is globe-trotting your passion?

♡ Will you take up any challenge offered to you?

♡ Do you live for new sights and sounds and tire quickly of the familiar?

♡ Do you make sure you get your own way, no matter what?

♡ Is one lover simply not enough?

If you're grabbing your suitcase, that sounds like a yes, so take the first flight to Borneo to continue your escapades.

Intellectual Temptress

Often the most dangerous sirens of all, intellectual temptresses seduce with their minds. Take Lou Andreas-Salomé, for instance …

Born in St Petersburg in 1861, Salomé was obsessed with learning from an early age. At seventeen, she persuaded a Dutch preacher to teach her theology and philosophy; he became obsessed with her and planned to divorce his wife. Salomé fled to Zurich to escape him.

Aged twenty-one, Salomé began a relationship with the philosopher Friedrich Nietzsche, who fell madly in love with her and went on to base some of his theories on her personality. They parted on bad terms, however, and Nietzsche never got over her. Salomé subsequently became a psychiatrist – and no less than Sigmund Freud found her the most stimulating woman he'd ever met.

Although she was against marriage, Salomé wed a linguistics scholar and enjoyed an open celibate relationship with him for forty years.

Do you seduce with your mind?

♡ Is your intellect your driving force?

♡ Does your curiosity enchant men?

♡ Are you as happy with a book as with a lover?

♡ Can you seduce with words and ideas?

♡ Are you a mental Medusa?

If you find yourself nodding wisely at these questions, it's pretty safe to assume you already know your own mind. But don't take life too seriously – intellectual temptresses take off their glasses and let their hair down when they stop working. Keep a pair of blue stockings handy …

Man-Eater

This is the most openly brazen of all seductresses. Singer and actress Grace Jones epitomizes this type: she is unique, bizarre and, according to her high school report, 'socially sick'.

Andy Warhol once told Grace she'd never make it without toning down her look. Instead, she toned it up and went on to become an icon of 1980s cult pop superstardom. 'I'm a man-eating machine,' she said, and she scared the hell out of a generation of males with her severe androgynous looks. Despite this, she's been married twice and counts Dolph Lundgren and an earl among her many boyfriends.

Grace doesn't just look scary; she *is* scary. In 1981, she slapped chat-show host Russell Harty across the face live on air, because she felt she was being ignored. The incident topped a 2006 BBC poll of the most shocking British TV chat-show moments.

Now well past the age she expected to die, on signing her latest record deal she famously said, 'Grrrrr!'

Do you eat men for breakfast?

♡ Do you devour men in your sleep?

♡ Can you match them drink for drink?

♡ Do you bare your teeth in the face of convention?

♡ Do you stamp on anyone who gets in your way?

♡ Is your personal magnetism so strong that it enslaves
men, even when you treat them like doormats?

If you're growling yes to all of these, it looks like you've
found your kind. Man-eaters wear jewels and fur, show
off their bodies, roar, prowl and prey on hapless males.

Domestic Goddess

> " Sometimes ... we don't want to feel like a post-modern, post-feminist, overstretched woman but, rather, a domestic goddess, trailing nutmeggy fumes of baking pie in our languorous wake ... "
>
> *Nigella Lawson*

With her jet-black hair, porcelain skin, ruby lips and curvy figure, Nigella has reintroduced glamour to the kitchen. Shimmying sexily around the cooker, she delights in seductive culinary creations. Who can resist her lusciousness as she fawns and fantasizes over chocolate-cake mix? Her unashamedly sensual attitude to food has turned cooking into a thoroughly sexy pursuit.

The daughter of a politician and an heiress, Nigella moved school nine times because she was 'difficult' and 'disruptive', and started her career as a book reviewer and restaurant critic. Her first cookery book sold 300,000 copies, even though she's not a trained chef or cook, and her second book won the British Book Award for Author of the Year. TV beckoned, and critics praised her relaxed, intimate approach to food; she was even dubbed the 'queen of food porn'.

'If it's something I don't want to carry on eating once I'm full, then I don't want the recipe,' she says.

Do you have Nigella's allure?

♡ Do men worship at your kitchen altar?

♡ Can you roast a chicken seductively?

♡ Do you look sexy in an apron?

♡ Are you the hostess with the mostest?

♡ Do you look saucy when you're eating?

Domestic goddesses wear cashmere cardigans under their aprons, high heels and red lipstick. Strawberries and chocolate are never far from their sensuous lips.

Vintage Vamps

> 66 It takes a hundred times more skill to make love than to command an army. 99
>
> *Ninon de Lenclos*, arch-temptress

Historically, all the great enchantresses have had an innate ability to make the world work for them. They bucked convention and invented their own moral codes. For most of them, marriage was out of the question; domesticity was abhorrent.

In short, the seductresses of bygone eras were inherently naughty, with a grand sense of 'me'. They were fascinating and they knew how to manipulate this for their own gain. Many of them were, of course, beautiful – this was their main currency in a world that often denied them the chance to earn a living outside prostitution.

But the love queens of history could not get by on beauty alone. Like Scheherazade in *1001 Arabian Nights*, who keeps the Sultan awake with her storytelling, the art of conversation was key to their seductive powers.

Sexpertise was often, but not always, another vital ingredient – however, no true seductress ever relied entirely on bedroom skills. Often the object of desire had to be kept in a continuous state of courtship. The very nature of the art was to attract, tease, love, withdraw and disappear, only then to reappear even more fascinating than before.

History's Hottest Heroines

Here are some of the most glorious and outrageous women from history, to help inspire you to discover the woman *you* want to be – and to stop you moulding yourself into someone society/men/everyone else tells you to be.

Madame de Pompadour (1721–1764)

Before she enchanted Louis XV of France and became his mistress, seducing him at a masked ball where she dressed as a shepherdess and he as a hedge, Madame Jeanne-Antoinette de Pompadour was Madame d'Étoiles

– married to her guardian's nephew. She was famous for her lively salons, frequented by some of the greatest minds of the age, including Voltaire, and where she developed her captivating conversational skills.

After she separated from her husband, Louis bought her the Pompadour title, without which she could not be presented at court. From her boudoir at the Palace of Versailles, she influenced court life and developed trendsetting styles of dress – and undress – including the negligée.

Jeanne-Antoinette was allegedly not keen on sex and so dosed herself with aphrodisiacs to keep up with the king's libido. However, she was passionate in her intellectual pursuits, including design and architecture, and most notably politics; she is often credited with helping bring about the Treaty of Versailles between France and Austria. After they ceased being lovers, she and Louis remained friends until her death from tuberculosis aged forty-two.

Lola Montez (1821–1861)

Irish-born Lola Montez, 'the Spanish dancer', was an infamous nineteenth-century seductress: full of life, good in bed and sparkling company, Montez was dubbed the 'man-killing spectacle' of Europe.

Undaunted by his reputation as one of the most desired men in Europe, or by his entourage of female admirers, Montez presented herself to Franz Liszt at a stage door one evening. They enjoyed a passionate affair, but she wore him out to the point that he could take no more, and he locked her in his hotel room and fled.

Later, she stormed the apartments of Ludwig I of Bavaria. It was rumoured that when the king asked if her breasts were real, she slashed her bodice open with a pair of scissors. The king claimed he was 'in a grip of passion like never before' but she left him a broken man when she absconded to Geneva sixteen months later.

Although married several times, Montez hated the thought of being tied down. 'I am a free independent being, subject to my whims and sensations alone.'

Her reckless attitude to love was not without its consequences, however – during a violent row, one of her lovers, who had left his wife to be with Lola on her tour of Australia, jumped overboard and drowned on their return journey. Deeply shocked, Montez stopped ravishing men and began lecturing on the art of seduction. But not before she had thrilled audiences with her erotic Spider Dance, with which she outraged respectable people by raising her skirts far, far too high.

Cora Pearl (1835–1886)

One of the most fiendishly naughty girls of the nineteenth century was Emma Elizabeth Crouch, a.k.a. Cora Pearl, a convent girl who fell by the wayside in London and became involved in sleazy prostitution before becoming a high-class courtesan.

When one of her lovers took her to Paris, she fell in love with the city, refused to return to England, changed her name and took to the stage – but made her main income from sex. Earning thousands of francs a night (the average wage was three francs a day), she became legendary for her antics, which included dancing naked on a carpet of orchids, bathing in champagne before an audience of dinner guests, and at one party even serving herself up on a massive dish, powdered with sugar and with a grape in her navel.

Delighting in causing shock, she threw outrageous transvestite balls, where she waltzed with her pet pig. Her activities drew a great deal of attention and soon she had the cream of Paris knocking at her front door; William, Prince of Orange, Gustave Dore, the Duc de Mornay, a Turkish emir and the emperor's brother, Prince Napoleon, all vied for her affections.

Eventually her love escapades got her into trouble. One of her boyfriends was so smitten and outraged by her cruel love games that he arrived at her house, loaded a gun in front of her and shot himself. Paris was so horrified that Cora was hounded out of town.

La Belle Otero (1868–1965)

Another nineteenth-century *femme fatale* was Spanish-born Caroline Otero – described by her lover Maurice Chevalier as 'the most dangerous woman of her time'. Six men committed suicide after being entangled with her, earning her an unenviable title: the Suicide Siren.

Caroline came from an impoverished family and was the victim of an abusive childhood. She ran away from home, hooked up with a dancer and learned Flamenco dancing. Moving to France at the age of twenty, she created the character of La Belle Otero and eventually became a dancer at Les Folies Bergère in Paris.

Otero's sultry beauty and elegant figure were legendary. Her breasts were said to precede her by a quarter of an hour when she entered a room. She refused to marry any of her wealthy suitors, declaring, 'I wasn't meant to be domesticated.' A self-made temptress from hell, she told a girlfriend that a man becomes yours not at the moment you spread your legs, but at the moment you twist his wrist.

Otero's wardrobe was the toast of the town. She was 'like a precious idol decked with gifts of the faithful'. All this she later squandered on gambling. Nevertheless, she lived to the grand old age of ninety-six.

How to Emulate the Love Queens

You might not have kings, dukes, philosophers and composers on hand to seduce, but that doesn't mean you can't work it like these world-class seductresses. All you need to do is:

♡ Cultivate your wit.

♡ Stuff convention.

♡ Extend your general knowledge.

♡ Learn the language (and look) of love.

♡ Garner a treasure trove of anecdotes and quips.

♡ Nurture the gift of the gab.

♡ Develop your opinions (no sheep here, please).

♡ Tread your own path.

♡ Have your own moral code (no, this isn't an excuse to trample on other women – they're your allies, remember).

Name That Siren *Quiz*

1. Which ultimate seductress wrapped herself in a carpet and smuggled herself into the palace of the Roman Emperor?

2. 'The sheer magic of her personality' had her suitors and courtiers on their knees. This Russian was the belle of the Thursday transvestite balls. Who was she?

3. Called the 'bewitching one', this English rose lived under one roof with four 'husbands'. She was a harpsichord and clavichord player of great repute, who had a wardrobe full of feather turbans and fishbone earrings. What was her name?

4. Which great comic actress told Charles II to 'lock up his codpiece' when she became his mistress?

5. Which French chanteuse declared: 'I'm ugly. I'm not Venus. I've got sagging breasts, a low-slung ass and drooping buttocks … but I can still get men!'

6. She was dubbed a 'female Don Juan' and claimed that 'old women are more beloved than younger women' – who was she?

7. Which older opera mezzo-soprano caught the heart of acclaimed author Ivan Turgenev, twenty years her junior?

8. Who was the 'Bronze Venus' who 'gave all of Paris a hard-on'?

9. She bagged the king of England, who had to abdicate the throne for her. He called her his 'oxygen'. Who was she?

10. The inspiration for Henry James's novel *Portrait of a Lady*, which art collector was the 'idol of men and the envy of women'?

Answers overleaf ...

Answers

1. Cleopatra
2. Catherine the Great
3. Violet Gordon Woodhouse
4. Nell Gwyn
5. Edith Piaf
6. George Sand
7. Pauline Viardot
8. Josephine Baker
9. Wallis Simpson
10. Isabella Stewart Gardener

If you haven't heard of some of these ladies, get reading – you could learn some invaluable lessons in naughtiness from their incredible lives.

Daily Doses

of Naughtiness

Playing at Work

> " There ought to be a better way
> to start the day than by getting
> up in the morning. "
>
> *Anon*

Unless you're blessed with your dream job and go skipping and singing to work every day, it can be hard to maintain a sense of fun when you head into the office. If flirting with the office hottie and getting the gossip around the water cooler aren't doing it for you – or, God forbid, aren't even a possibility – you need some tricks up your sleeve to add some zest to the nine-to-five.

How to Go to Work

It's all about attitude – and letting the bastards grind you
down is categorically *not* an option. The key is to rebel
in subtle ways – just enough to make you feel that you,
and not the powers-that-be, are in control of your office
life, but not so much that you get yourself fired. Here are
some suggestions to get your imagination going:

♡ It's not easy being nice if you can't stand your
boss, but it's a lot easier if you've got 'SCREW
YOU!' written across your chest in felt tip (hidden
under your shirt or blouse, of course). Taking a
deep breath every time the chief annoys you will
simultaneously calm you down and push your
invisible insult to the fore.

♡ Wear a full-on vampish black lace knickers, bra and
suspenders combo underneath your work clothes
every now and then. Whether your colleagues
are male or female, your naughty little secret
will amuse you throughout the day and may well
empower you in unexpected ways.

♡ Address hated colleagues using swear words
concealed within perfectly ordinary-sounding
sentences, for example: 'Are you going out fu-

coffee?' or 'Have you got a spare piss of paper?'
You must not smirk or giggle, or they will notice.
Save the laughter for later.

♡ Remember that office-outing group photo you
hated so much? Get yourself ten copies right now
to take home with you at the end of the day.
When you need to express hatred for your boss or
colleagues, all you need to do is cut out the head
of the offending party, draw a comedy cock or
pair of breasts and stick the head on your drawing.
It sounds stupid, but that's the point; it works so
well because you can't help but laugh – at them
and yourself. You'll still be amused the next day at
work, taking the sting out of their behaviour.

♡ Make your excuses interesting – whether for being
late, leaving early or having a long lunch – such
as: 'The bus engine burst into flames'; 'The man
upstairs threw himself out of the window and I had
to give him mouth-to-mouth to revive him'; 'I'm
meeting an inheritance lawyer about the death of a
long-lost relative who left me her millions.'

> " Always be smarter than the
> people who hire you. "
> *Lena Horne*, US singer and actress

What to Keep in Your Handbag

You need all the stimulation you can get to reach Friday night, ladies – here are your essentials:

Erotic literature

Ideal for perking you up on the way in to work, or for getting you in the mood on your way to a date, or for allowing fantasies to engulf you on long train journeys.

Dominatrix

Carry a retractable whip with telescopic folding action for handbag-sized control whenever you need it!

Spanking paddle

Essential for all those naughty boys out there who need a good old-fashioned spanking.

Lipstick vibrator

It looks like it goes on your lips, but it doesn't … perfect for a quick pick-me-up in the loo.

How *Not* to Go to Work (In Other Words, How to Throw a Sickie)

If, even when armed with your new naughty ways of getting through the daily grind, it is still too much to bear, you might find yourself tempted into what is technically known as 'doing a bunk'. Even the thought of it makes you feel like a badly behaved schoolgirl, which, let's face it, can be rather delicious. A note of caution, however: this does have to be limited to absolutely *desperate* moments or you'll end up like the boy who cried wolf – no one will believe you and the big bad boss will gobble you up. So follow these instructions and proceed with caution …

The set-up

Trick 1. Act ill the day before. Mope around listlessly, saying, 'I just don't feel myself today!' Fake the odd dizzy spell by making yourself light-headed thinking about how fantastic it would be to have a few paid days off.

Trick 2. Make your face pale. A faint layer of green concealer (usually used to neutralize red blemishes) works wonders.

Trick 3. Fake a fever. Put a thermometer against the radiator when no one's looking. Rub your face vigorously or find an empty office and stand on your head for two minutes to make your face look flushed. Hide some self-heating gloves in your handbag; make frequent visits to the loo and use them to heat up your face.

Trick 4. Laugh weakly at people's jokes. Make out that you're a trooper soldiering on, trying to keep it together and be normal.

Trick 5. Make sure a colleague overhears you cancelling tonight's social engagement because you don't feel all that great and want to get an early night.

Trick 6. Brush your hand wearily over your face from time to time.

Trick 7. If you're faking a cold, breathe in and out through your mouth all day, as if you're bunged up. Fake the odd sneeze and pathetic cough. Say, 'Brrr, it's cold in here!' and put on an extra layer or two of clothing.

N.B. It can be useful to set up a recurring illness that colleagues will instantly accept without question: 'It's another kidney infection', 'My allergies are playing up again' or 'I think it might be another migraine'.

The sting

Option 1. Think sad thoughts and ring up work whispering about your bad stomach/sore throat/achy bones. If you're lying down, you'll sound extra groggy. Don't say, 'If I feel better, I'll try and come in later,' as it's a dead giveaway. Don't even think about feeling guilty – it's your right to be ill sometimes, even when you're not.

Option 2. Look up the symptoms of bubonic plague and start describing them in graphic detail, saying, 'I just don't know what it could be!'

Option 3. Just say, 'Really bad diarrhoea, all night ... You don't want to know ... Oh no, not again! I'd better go now, *right now.*' Or croak, 'Look, I would come in, but the doctor says it's really contagious.' Or if you have a male boss, cite 'women's problems' – he will be as eager to get off the phone as you are, unless he is a gynaecologist.

Option 4. Sprinkle flour in your mouth and roll out your excuse, dry-mouthed, coughing every now and then.

Say you've called the doctor and you're waiting for a call back.

Option 5. Send an email from your flatmate's email account (with his/her permission, of course), saying that you're too ill to phone or write yourself. Keep it short, do it early.

The pay-off

It's priceless! The time is yours to do whatever you damn well choose. Three days in the South of France – yippee! – but turn your phone off at all times, or the foreign ring will give you away, and don't get a tan. Or how about a nice day shopping – it's guaranteed to put a spring in your step, though you should wait a good week before you wear your new shoes to work. Or why not take a couple of days in your trackies watching daytime telly and eating ice cream? Better yet, have lots and lots of illicit sex (just don't answer the phone while you're at it).

The Naughty Guide to Money

Let's face it, there are two basic approaches to money: spend or save. We are all naturally inclined to do either one or the other, so which camp do you fall into – the piggy-bank lover or the piggy-piggy big spender?

The Savings Saint

Saving money can be fun if you think in the long term, unless you're the type of good girl who scrimps every penny and leaves millions of pounds to the local cat or donkey refuge (although that would be one in the eye for your grasping relatives). You, oh virtuous one, save up assiduously until you've retired, then go on a glamorous cruise and bag yourself a twenty-five-year-old toyboy in the Caribbean. Go Granny, go! Here's how ...

How to save millions

Live on noodles, beans and evaporated milk, and avoid all potentially dangerous activities to ensure longevity. Limit your alcohol intake to one glass of sherry a year and make your own Christmas cards. You might lose all your friends and find the neighbourhood cats moving in with you, but just think of all the pennies saved! Or, more to the point, what you can do with those pennies ...

How to find a toyboy

So you've now stashed away a fortune and are living in far-flung exotic climes – the next step is to fix yourself up with a young hottie. Saunter into a beach bar, buy a bottle of expensive liquor and tell the barman you want to learn how to salsa. Keep flashing the cash, avoid flashing too much wrinkled flesh, and Bob's your uncle. Or your new toyboy …

The Spendthrift Sinner

You can live for the moment, spend spend spend and let tomorrow look after itself, hoping that a sugar daddy will save you from the wreckage. Or, alternatively, you can think ahead and find yourself a billionaire patron *before* you start spending – ideally a childless widower or an older gent who delights in the whims and frivolities of feckless youth – and spend his money on designer clothes and trips to Venice.

How to find a sugar daddy

Doll yourself up, go to a posh hotel bar with a friend, show off your legs and be saucily cheeky to any silverbacks who try to chat to you. They'll be grateful for the attention and you'll be grateful for the free drinks/food – and, if you're utterly shameless, clothes/cars/houses. If you need some tips on flirting, go to page 92.

How to find a billionaire patron

Advertise yourself as a house-sitter in *Tatler* or *Harper's*; wangle an invite to a big art opening and faint in the arms of a bigwig; nurse a pathetic cup of tea in Fortnum and Mason or Claridges and let a single teardrop run down your pretty, young, mournful cheek. Some benevolent old toff is bound to approach. Keep your necklines low, your hemlines high, your sob story going, and with any luck the cash will start flowing, you naughty hussy.

All Spent

Renowned beauty and actress Lily Langtry enchanted Edward Prince of Wales (later Edward VII) after he arranged to sit next to her at a dinner party given by a friend. Edward built them a weekend retreat in Bournemouth called Red House (now Langtry Manor) and allowed her to design it. But he complained about how much money she frittered away. Apparently he moaned, 'I've spent enough on you to build a battleship.' Whereupon she replied, 'And you've spent enough *in* me to float one.' Saucy! They broke up after three years when she went off with an earl, and then another prince, and then an old friend.

Minxing the Shops

> 66 I love to shop after a bad relationship …
> I buy a new outfit and it makes me feel better.
> Sometimes I see a really great outfit, I'll break
> up with someone on purpose. 99
>
> *Rita Rudner*, US comedienne

Shopping can be a real drag. Pushy assistants, the wrong colours, sizes and your imperfect bum can all contribute to the pain of trawling the retail world for something that actually fits and looks good.

But shopping can also really perk a girl up if she knows how to make the most of it. Going with a naughty best friend is recommended, preferably after a small brunch and a champagne cocktail (just one, mind, or you're asking for retail trouble).

Here's how to minx the shops:

♡ Take a poster of Marilyn Monroe (size 16 and wobbly!) into the changing room with you and blu-tack it to the mirror. Alternatively, take a lipstick and draw a big pair of lips on the mirror. Self-loathing is the enemy of naughty girls, OK? Got cellulite? So what! You've got a brain too, which is more than can be said of most of the pale-faced sticks who feature in magazine fashion shoots.

♡ Confuse the changing-room attendant by asking for your number tags in multiples. So if you're taking in seven items of clothing, say, 'Sorry, seven is my unlucky number. Can I take a three and a four instead?' Watch their expressions as they try to work out whether it's a scam or not. Hours of fun!

♡ Go into a really expensive shop and pick out the most ghastly comedy item of clothing you can find, try it on and encourage the staff to tell you how great you look in it. Get your friend in on the act and you'll giggle for the rest of the day.

♡ Don't take shopping too seriously, even if you've absolutely got to find something for tonight's party. Nice clothes are like men: they have a habit of hiding from you if you search for them too aggressively. And beware – shop assistants can smell desperation and will be delighted to capitalize on it.

♡ Assistants get excited when you pick out the most expensive clothes in the shop and try them on. Who are you to deny them the odd frisson of anticipation at the thought of your platinum credit card? You'll feel like a queen trying on all those posh frocks, so everybody wins. Never apologize for not buying. Just thank them for their help and they'll go on thinking you're the real thing as you head for the nearest charity shop.

♡ Split the cost of an expensive purchase across two or more bank accounts or credit cards. This way you won't feel you've spent so much money.

♡ Shopping with boyfriends, partners or husbands is worse than being stuck in a two-foot cabin on a raging sea. Avoid at all costs! Shop only with your naughtiest girlfriends and insist they tell the truth.

♡ Tell the truth back, but never mention the 'fat' word. 'Unflattering' covers a multitude of flaws, from fat to old to grossly misshapen, and we all know what it really means. So, be kind, be only moderately honest and keep the best clothes for yourself. Meeeooww.

♡ Don't apologize when you take something back. If asked why you don't want an item, say, 'None of your business! I am merely exercising my statutory rights.' (Make sure you do it within twenty-eight days though, or your smart-arsed face will be burning with blushes afterwards.)

♡ Put your new purchases in the back of your cupboard and bring them out slowly, thus avoiding sartorial ennui and awkward questions ('Yet *another* new skirt?').

Truth or Dare

Lying is bad. We all know that. But there's nothing wrong with a little bit of hoodwinking from time to time, is there? The occasional flight of fancy can add all kinds of spice to life. Here's how to go for a spin on the truth and falsehood merry-go-round …

How to Tell Fibs

Step 1. Firstly, decide whether it's worth the effort. Are you risking too much for the last doughnut in the fridge?

Step 2. Figure out exactly what you're going to say and stick to it. Think through the questions you may be asked and work out how to answer them.

Writing down your fib will help you remember it when the time comes to do the naughty deed: 'That doughnut was going off, so I threw it away.'

Step 3. Visualize the made-up events actually happening, from your disgusted face as you spot the patch of mould on the doughnut to the angry toss with which you bin it. That way, you'll appear to be remembering what happened.

Step 4. Build a believable story around your fib. 'I'd just come out of the bath and I was feeling thirsty, but when I went to the fridge, there was nothing in there except a stale doughnut.'

Step 5. Destroy the evidence and make sure there's nothing left to incriminate you. (Empty the bin and check for sugar or jam around your lips.)

Step 6. Don't avoid eye contact – it's really suspicious. Look them straight in the eye and believe in what you're saying: 'Yes, a greeny sort of patch of bacteria!'

Step 7. Don't smile too much. Fibbing makes you nervous and nervous people often smile or giggle to relieve tension. Relax – fidgeting and sweating are dead giveaways.

Step 8. Keep your palms at your side, and leave them there, because fibbers tend to touch their noses and their mouths unconsciously when they tell porkies. Policemen often make small talk with people to establish 'normal' behaviour. Then, when they get down to the serious subject matter of missing doughnuts, they look for deviation from that behaviour.

Step 9. Keep a steady voice and don't protest too much. Act like you don't care whether the person believes you or not. 'I wouldn't blame you for thinking I'd scarfed it, because I love doughnuts.' Don't get defensive: it's a childishly obvious symptom of guilt.

Step 10. Throw a half-truth into the mix. 'Actually, I was going to eat it and pretend it had gone off, but then I realized that it *had* gone off. That'll teach me, won't it?' (Inner smirk – did I just get away with that?)

Telling Tall Tales

Add a flourish to your stories by incorporating any of the following elements in your dinner-party conversations:

♡ The son of a Maharajah

♡ Royal jelly

♡ A diamond the size of a man's fist

♡ The Lost City of the Incas

♡ A tame baby tiger

♡ A swarm of killer bees

♡ Sexual tricks involving a silk scarf and a silver dollar

♡ A revolving bed

Ridiculous Party Lines

If you find yourself staring into the bottom of yet another empty glass of bubbly, while your ears are assaulted by the monotone drone of someone you stopped listening to about twenty minutes ago, ditch the bore and try to liven things up by injecting some absurdities into your conversation ...

Party Guest: How do you know the host?
You: *He/she saved me from a great white shark attack.*

Party Guest: What do you do for a living?
You: *I'm a bomb-disposal expert.*

Party Guest: What are you drinking?
You: *Schnapps and snake sweat.*

Party Guest: Where do you live?
You: *In a grace-and-favour apartment at Clarence House, but it's only temporary, thank goodness.*

Party Guest: How are you getting home?
You: *My father's picking me up in his pony and trap before he starts his rag-and-bone round.*

Party Guest: What are you doing for the rest of the weekend?
You: *A trapeze and fire-eating seminar.*

Party Guest: How do you relax?
You: *By getting drunk and spouting nonsense.*

Let's Get
Physical

Getting Fit the Naughty Way

It's hard to imagine the highly elegant actress Joanna Lumley wearing rubber gloves (except perhaps reprising the role of outrageous party-girl Patsy in *Absolutely Fabulous*, in some fantastically deviant scenario, that is …). And yet she has declared that she doesn't mind the slog of household chores, because, she says, 'Each time I do it, I think, this is instead of going to the gym.' So why not take a fag out of Patsy's packet and forget the goody-goody treadmill? There are far more productive and satisfying ways to shape up – just follow these nicely saucy suggestions.

Give Your Gym the Slip

Here are some ways to shed pounds without pounding away in front of other Sweaty Bettys.

Perfect the 1950s wiggle

Not for nothing did they call the pencil skirt the 'Wiggle' skirt back in the 1950s. Make like a latter-day goddess and get those hips working – gyrate your way round the bedroom, through the boardroom, and work the high street like a couture catwalk.

Fact: Wiggling your hips and jiggling around uses up to 250 calories an hour.

Get fit in the fitting room

How fun and easy is this one? Imagine the kilojoules you can shed simply trying on clothes: stepping in and out of trousers and skirts; stretching to do up dress zips, pulling on tops. It's step, yoga and weights all in one!

Fact: You lose 144 calories an hour pushing a trolley around the supermarket. Add the time spent walking from shop to shop and that's enough fitness for one day.

Chase boys … chase boys … chase boys …

Boys are such a distraction – even thinking about them makes you slimmer. Why waste time on aerobics? Instead, get out and visit that man: you'll be fitter by the time you get there (if you don't scoff a cake on the way).

Fact: Walking burns four calories a minute. If you choose a guy who lives at least thirty minutes from your house, you'll lose at least 120 calories just going to visit him.

Think about it

Clever girls, rejoice; the more you think, the more calories you use. So galvanize that grey matter and keep fit thinking up ways to be naughty. Keep a diary of all the fun you're having; compose a dirty limerick; write a saucy letter to your lover; or simply try to budget your spending (arggh!) – all of it will help keep you trim.

Fact: Thinking hard uses one and a half calories a minute.

Dance, pretty lady, dance!

Turn your lounge into your very own nightclub room by dimming the lights, cranking up your favourite tunes and grooving to the music for thirty minutes. This is FUN, so go for it.

Fact: You burn 350–400 calories per hour dancing – and three calories for every minute you laugh.

The horizontal workout

Would anyone go to the gym if they knew that having energetic sex five days a week is the equivalent of two and half hours working out? Thirty minutes of sex burns more than 200 calories. And it's good for your heart in more ways than one. People who have sex three times a week have a fifty per cent lower risk of suffering a heart attack or stroke. 'Sex without love is merely healthy exercise,' said the sci-fi writer Robert A. Heinlein. What does he mean, *merely*?!

Fact: Saucy ladies will be pleased to know that the more audacious you are while having sex and the more daring you are about where you have sex can make a calorific difference:

Back of a car	220 calories per 30 mins
Back of a car in a busy car park	230 calories per 30 mins
In the park at twilight	240 calories per 30 mins
In an aeroplane loo	280 calories per 30 mins
In the park in daylight	290 calories per 30 mins
On an aeroplane, window seat	300 calories per 30 mins
Upstairs at your parents' house	300 calories per 30 mins

Sleep it off

After a hectic day thinking, chasing boys, dancing round the TV and having adventurous sex, you'll flop into bed only to find a good twelve-hour sleep will make you slimmer, more beautiful and ready for another day minxing around.

Fact: For every twelve hours you sleep, you lose a good few hundred calories! So let no man or mum call you a sloth. You're in bed busy shaping up, thanks very much.

Dirty Dancing

Women have always used the seductive power of dance to attract and enslave men. From as early as 300 BC they've caused havoc with their gyrating bodies, firing up a storm of testosterone and orgiastic delight. Got hips? Then use them to get yourself in the mood, dance him into the bedroom and satisfy your deepest desires. Don't worry if you haven't got an audience – dancing alone can be every bit as sexy as a prelude to a spot of auto-pleasure. Want to awaken your dancing devilishness? Here's how …

Burlesque

Burlesque originated in the vaudeville theatres of the nineteenth century. It was a combination of sexual satire and performance art. Over the decades it has developed into high-class striptease, with glamorous and suggestive props. To be a queen of burlesque you need to cultivate a love of dance, theatre, style and, of course, fashion.

For a sensuous striptease, every burlesque wannabe needs a pair of tasseled pasties (nipple covers), an easily removable lacy corset, a sexy g-string, long black gloves, a suspender belt and stockings, a pair of high-heeled shoes and a fan or feather boa. Don't forget to make up your face like a Hollywood starlet. Burlesque is all about glamour and feeling divine. And no matter what size or shape you may be, *never* hide your curves. Be proud of your body and don't be afraid to show it off. Here is a handful of the basic burlesque moves:

♡ **The Shimmy:** stand with your legs slightly apart, then in quick succession bend your left knee slightly, then your right knee slightly, and repeat again and again.

♡ **The Quiver:** throw your shoulders back and shake, shake, shake!

♡ **The Innocent Reveal:** let a strap or an item of clothing slip off and accidentally-on-purpose reveal some flesh.

♡ **The Bump and Grind:** shift your hip to one side on a musical beat and then rotate your pelvis.

♡ **The Shock:** widen your eyes and purse your lips, as if you can't believe what you've just done.

Dita Von Teese

The world's first erotic superstar, born Heather Renée Sweet in 1972, Dita Von Teese is the queen of burlesque and a muse to fashion designers, who applaud her elegant style. With her delicate white skin, jet-black hair, rose-red lips and deliciously curvy figure, she's reminiscent of a dreamy 1940s starlet, and was particularly inspired by Betty Grable. She started stripping at eighteen after studying ballet and theatrical costume design, and went on to do glamour and fetish modelling, before turning to burlesque in the 1990s. Her burlesque strip shows are witty and accomplished, featuring such props as a giant martini glass, a horse and a bathtub. She is in demand throughout the world.

Pole Dancing

Pole dancing originated in the early 1900s as part of the burlesque striptease show. Revived in the 1960s by a dancer named Belle Jangles at a strip bar in Oregon, it took off as a craze in the 1980s. Get into action with these simple steps …

Step 1. Start by walking around the pole. Stand up straight and push your bum and chest out. Link the pole into the crook of your arm and begin to strut around it.

Step 2. Next perform what's called the **Bridge**. You hold the pole with one hand and straddle it between your legs. Then bend your knees and arch your back until you can see behind you.

Step 3. Now for the **Ripple**. Grip the pole with one hand and lean forward onto it until your shoulder is touching it. Stick your bum out and move your tummy towards the pole until it touches it. Slowly pull your shoulders back and feel the pole between your legs.

Step 4. Think you can do the **Leg Grip** next? Hold the pole with two hands, jump up and grab it with your legs. Grip tightly. Stretch out one leg while bending the other leg and rotate around the pole.

Step 5. Then there's the **Reverse Hold**. Standing side-on to the pole, grab it with two hands again, but keeping your arms stretched out above your head. Get the pole in the crease of your right leg and, with your feet crossed behind you, rotate enticingly around it.

Belly Dancing

Equally seductive, belly dancing requires physical stamina, but is less acrobatic than pole dancing. Originally performing for women only, belly dancers wore layers of clothing, showing no skin. The rhythmic movements of the dance made the material bounce playfully. In 1930s Egypt, bare bellies emerged, causing a sensation. In 1950, politicians put a stop to this erotic naked navel gazing, but public outrage led to the ban being repealed, with the stipulation that dancers would once again cover their stomachs. Today, belly dancing is a means of celebrating femininity. Plus, when it comes to childbirth, women who belly dance have shorter labours – what a bonus!

One of the best things about belly dancing are the outrageous costumes. A veil is key. Headbands, necklaces, bracelets and arm cuffs are all great accessories. To dance with the veil, lift up your head, relax your shoulders, and stick your chest out. Hold the veil between your thumb and fingers and treat it like an extension of your arms.

Most belly dancing is derived from the following twelve movements – the names are self-explanatory.

♡ Hip twist
♡ Hip in and out
♡ Hip drop and lift

♡ Hip circle

♡ Vertical hip circle

♡ Figure of eight hip circle

♡ Diagonal chest circle

♡ Horizontal chest circle

♡ Vertical chest circle

♡ Arm undulations

♡ Shoulder shimmy

♡ Head slide

Dance of the Seven Veils

Traditionally associated with Salome (see page 70), this infamous strip dance is thought to have originated in Babylonian mythology, a story in which the goddess Ishtar is tricked into removing an item of clothing at each of the seven gates to the underworld (that old chestnut!). It's been written about, performed and filmed a thousand times, but how do you actually do it? Of course, no one knows for certain, but here are some suggestions:

Step 1. First you need seven scarves of varying size and fabric – including silk, chiffon and gauze – easily found in any market for a few pounds.

Step 2. Now wrap a small scarf around your hips to make a mini-skirt and criss-cross another around your breasts to make a bandeau.

Step 3. Next, tie a larger scarf or kanga around your waist, over the mini, and a floaty scarf over the bandeau. That's four scarves so far!

Step 4. Tie a very small silk scarf around one thigh, like a garter, and another around your upper arm. One final, large flowing scarf should cover you from breasts to ankles. Be careful not to tie them too tight or you'll spend too long fiddling around trying to undo them. Equally, tie them too loose and they'll fall off as you're dancing!

Step 5. Put some music on and undulate, waving your arms around exotically while you slowly slip off each scarf and drop it tantalizingly to the floor.

Salome

According to the Bible, Salome pleased King Herod Antipas so greatly when she danced for him that he offered her whatever she wanted. Instead of saying, 'OK, I'll have a house, some horses and lots of fabulous robes,' she went off to ask her mother's advice. Herodias, her mum, who had a grudge against John the Baptist, told her to ask Herod Antipas for John the Baptist's head. So that's what she did, stupid girl! Still, no one would have remembered her or her alluring Dance of the Seven Veils if she hadn't. John the Baptist was beheaded and his head presented to the unfortunate Salome, who by then was probably wishing that she had asked for a nice bottle of scent.

Music to strip to

'The Stripper' by David Rose & His Orchestra
'Je t'aime' by Serge Gainsbourg and Jane Birkin
'Samba Saravah' by Baden Powell
'After the Dance' by Marvin Gaye
'Strangers in the Night' by Acker Bilk
'Come on Closer' by Jem

'Feeling Good' by Nina Simone (covered by Muse and Michael Bublé among others)
'Brown Sugar' by D'Angelo
'Apple Suite Bass Theme' by Rick Dickert
'Sidewalk Blues' by Jelly Roll Morton
'Funky Blues' by Charlie Parker

Gypsy Rose Lee

Born in 1913, Rose Louise Hovick was considered to be a pretty lacklustre performer until she developed her burlesque strip show, which became legendary. Hugely witty, she chatted to her audience while she teased them with her act and became as famous for her onstage banter as her strip style. After being arrested numerous times by the police while performing in New York, she eventually made her way to Hollywood, where she wowed LA with her high-class strip act, often giving intellectual recitations while she whipped off her clothes.

Picasso, Miro, Chagall and Ernst all gave her pictures, which adorned the walls of her LA home, and in 1941 she wrote a novel entitled *The G-String Murders*, which went on to be made into a film starring Barbara Stanwyck!

Exotic Dance *Quiz*

1. Name the dance style that came from Indian gypsies who migrated to Europe in the sixteenth century. At its heart is the *canta*, the song.

2. Which type of dance has its roots in avoiding bad breath? The jerky head movements were essential to avoid breathing each other's halitosis …

3. This dance came from the slaves who were transported from Africa in the sixteenth century. It was a sex pantomime danced with exaggerated hip movements and with an aggressive stance on the part of the man and a defensive stance on the part of the woman. What is it?

4. It was declared legal in America in 1999 as long as the woman stayed at least twelve inches away from the man. No 'frottage' (genital touching) was allowed – can you guess what dance it is?

5. It first appeared in the working-class ballrooms of Montparnasse in Paris in around 1830, and was originally a dance for couples, who indulged in high kicks and other gestures with arms and legs. Its name in French means 'scandal' – which dance is it?

6. These dancers came into being in the thirteenth century to perform a dance inspired by the famous Sufi poet, Rumi. The dance ceremony was called a *Sema*, which represents a mystical journey of man's spiritual ascent through mind and love to 'The Perfect'. Who were they?

7. Who were the erotic dancers who danced in cages in discos during the 1960s and whose dance was famous in a Los Angeles Venue called Whisky a Go Go?

Answers

1. Flamenco
2. Tango
3. Rumba
4. Lap dancing
5. The Can Can
6. Whirling Dervishes
7. Go Go Dancers

Cheeky Cosmetics

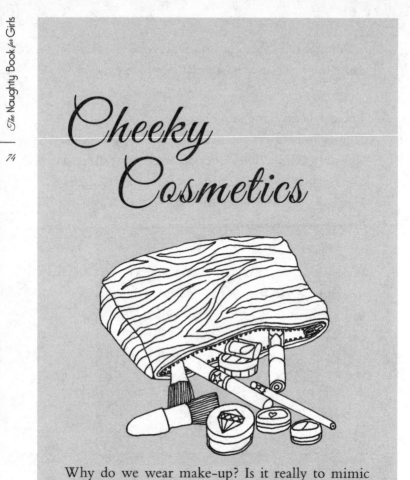

Why do we wear make-up? Is it really to mimic the flushed, wide-eyed look of arousal and orgasm, as is so often claimed? Or is it simply about trying to look younger or prettier? Is it an expression of creativity? Or do we wear make-up because the cosmetics industry tells us to? Whatever the reason, most of us can't live without our liner and lippy.

Did You Know?

♡ The word *cosmetae* was first used to describe Roman slaves who bathed men and women in perfume? Surely every girl needs one!

♡ The average modern woman spends just over £185,000 on beauty treatments in her lifetime. How naughty is that?

Hot Lips

The Ancient Egyptians added colour to their lips, cheeks and nails by grinding red ochre clay and mixing it with water. Men also wore make-up, but they didn't take their make-up jars along to parties, as women did. It was an essential item of burial equipment for both sexes, however, and the Pharaoh Tutankhamun was among those who carried eye make-up into the afterlife.

Cleopatra's lipstick was custom-made from crushed carmine beetles, which provided the red tint, and ants' eggs, which formed the base. By the time Elizabeth I was reddening her lips, lipstick was made from beeswax and plant dye. Shimmering lipsticks were originally created using an extract of fish scales known as pearlescence.

A rather alarming fact for all lipstick-wearers – lippy-loving women swallow between two and four kilos of lipstick in their lifetime! So stop licking your lips!

The Eyes Have It

Eyeliner

Kohl, a cosmetic made variously from soot, burnt almonds, ash, malachite and oxidized copper, was first used in Ancient Egypt as a protection against eye ailments. Darkening the eyelids also helped lessen the effects of sun glare and was thought to ward off the evil eye.

Wearing thick eyeliner on one eye and none on the other is a declaration of bisexuality (or scatty forgetfulness – whoops!).

Mascara

Rich Ancient Greeks had their mascara applied for them by dedicated make-up artists. The Gauls mixed garfish extract with soot and rubbed it on their lashes. The first commercial mascara was produced by nineteenth-century London perfumer Eugene Rimmel – yes, that's the same Rimmel that's now a global cosmetics company.

Modern mascara was invented just before World War I when chemist T.L. Williams mixed coal dust and Vaseline and named it Maybelline, after his sister Mabel.

Blushing Beauties

In Ancient Greece, people stained their cheeks and lips with mulberry juice. Other ancient cultures experimented with beetroot and strawberries.

Rouge was distinctly unfashionable for many centuries in Britain, because rosy cheeks suggested a life of outdoor labour, while a pale complexion spoke of luxury. However, this changed in the eighteenth century, with new lead- and mercury-based foundations, which had the unfortunate effect of seeping into their brains and driving them mad or fatally poisoning them.

A flushed appearance does give you an instant youthful look, and hints at a saucy post-coital glow, but beware of pinching your cheeks for a quick natural blush effect like Scarlett O'Hara in *Gone With the Wind* – it bursts capillaries and encourages spots!

Licentious Lingerie

For centuries, women have been seducing men
with sexy underwear, lace, feathers and frills –
and some helpful soft lighting. A sensual smile is
never far from your lips when you're wearing some
racy lingerie.

The Basics

If you're new to the pleasures of lingerie, here are the standard pieces that you might want to indulge in …

The suspender belt

When suspenders were first introduced in 1906, they were so unpopular they were withdrawn from the market. Now they are an indispensable sex aid! Why men fall for these fiddly contraptions is a mystery, but sometimes it's best not to ask questions. They've been compared to symbolic chastity belts, when really they're just a bit of lacy criss-cross sexy fun. The mere sight of them tends to make men fall at your feet, so who's complaining? Red and black are the classic colours, but any colour will do, especially pink with ribbons.

The garter

Garters were used to hold up stockings and socks before suspender belts were invented, but now they're simply a frivolous, cheeky thigh decoration. A lacy garter worn at the top of your stocking evokes Parisian dancers and naughty French boudoirs; the key to its appeal is often its removal. Traditionally, a bridegroom whips off his wife's garter and tosses it to the male wedding guests –

a practice still popular today. Why? The bride's clothes were historically thought to bring good luck, prompting guests to rip pieces off her dress; throwing the garter and the bride's bouquet were attempts to prevent the total ruination of her outfit!

Hold-ups

Hold-ups are magic stockings; they come off beautifully, without all the unclipping and flying straps of suspenders. There's something very sexy about the upper part of the thigh and they accentuate the creaminess of that bit of skin, whether they come in black, red or flesh. A pair of hold-ups accessorized with a pair of long black gloves, known as *mousquetaires* – and nothing else – can look elegant, and irresistibly sexy.

Corsets and basques

In the 1980s, Vivienne Westwood reinvented the restrictive Victorian corset by making it easier to put on and take off, and turning it into outerwear. Cinching in the waist and accentuating the breasts, today's basque is another essential item for the naughty wardrobe, evoking the burlesque era and combining blatant sexuality with echoes of social respectability. A classic black satin basque with ties up the back works every time – feel the delicious suspense while it's being undone.

The silky slip

Wearing silk against your skin always feels luxurious. Its cool smoothness makes it the most sensuous of fabrics.

The baby doll

Looking cute and girly gets you everywhere, especially if the night before you were dressed up in full-on dominatrix gear! Keep 'em guessing! Wear your baby doll nightie with matching puff panties and gaze up at him through your eyelashes. Pink is best; it's the colour of femininity because it evokes the flesh, apparently.

Backless panties

Pants that show off the place where your buttocks meet can be extremely saucy, especially when they're made of satin and tie up in a sweet bow.

The g-string

It's been a decade since low-cut jeans ushered in an era of derrière décolletage, or flashing your bum and thong, as it's more commonly known. Once shocking, they're now a practical item for clothes with a VPL problem, so long as you don't cross the line from sexy to trashy by revealing them above your jeans. They look great if you've got a fab butt.

For the More Adventurous

Crotchless knickers and nipple-less bras

Sometimes it's empowering to keep your underwear on when you're on top, especially if you're at all worried about what your boobs look like from that angle! Either way, crotchless knickers and nipple-less bras offer instant access if you're in a passionate fury, and there's no messing with clasps or twisting up your pants. They come in pretty sophisticated styles these days, too.

Pasties

Pasties are small, circular, cup-shaped pieces of material, which stick on to the nipple. They first emerged in the modern dance hall during the early 1920s when they were all the rage in Parisian dance halls, and they came back into fashion in the 1980s. Get yourself a pair with silk tassels or sequins, or shaped into red hearts. Hilarious and fun!

Rubber lingerie

The texture of thin rubber can be a real turn-on and it fits on the body like a second skin. Rubber and whips go together well, but be gentle, pussycat – it's just for show, unless you're both into the pain game.

Masks

Now you see me, now you don't ... Masks are mysterious, liberating and more than a tiny bit kinky, guaranteed to notch up the naughty factor.

> 66 If God wanted us to be naked, why did he invent sexy lingerie?
>
> *Shannon Doherty*, US actress 99

How Big are Your Panties?

Big pants

You don't care what people think of you as long as you feel comfortable. You're more at home with your granny than your boyfriend.

G-string

You're not afraid of the obvious and you've got a great bum. You are an extrovert and you don't mind people seeing you naked.

Briefs

You like to feel comfortable and sexy, but you're not prepared to suffer for it. You're confident in your own sexuality and you don't need to flaunt it.

French knickers

The way French knickers cut across your buttocks but flow loose around the thighs makes them sexy and breezy, just like you.

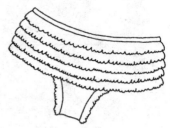

No pants

You're so damn hot you don't need to read this book. Marilyn Monroe would have been proud of you – she didn't wear pants either (and she wore her clothes extra tight so everyone knew it).

Fashion for Passion

> " I dress for the image. Not for myself,
> not for the public, not for fashion,
> not for men. "
>
> *Marlene Dietrich*

It's easy to forget that clothes should be fun and about what you want, not what magazines/men/sales assistants tell you to wear. So reclaim your wardrobe and start dressing to please that all-important style guru – YOU. If you want to look seductive and sexy, you have to wear clothes that you feel express you best. Here are some pointers for clothes that have passed the test of time for making women feel gorgeous – no matter what size or shape.

The Pencil Skirt

Whether you're curvy or skinny, the pencil skirt gives you a dangerously alluring walk thanks to the way it gathers in at the knee. It makes it impossible to take gallumphing man-strides, so you walk using daintier steps, which puts a swing into your hips and a wiggle in your glorious derrière.

The Little Black Dress

There's a bewildering array of options on the high street when it comes to picking out a glitzy dress for parties and swanky events. That padded-shoulder sequinned affair might knock 'em dead today (and in twenty years' time when it comes round again) but if you want a dress you can rely on to make you come over all Audrey Hepburn, and which you can whip out time and again, the classic LBD is your trusty friend. It's slimming, classy and guaranteed to boost your confidence.

Silk

Combining the sensual feeling of silk next to your skin with the fact that it is often slightly see-through (but make sure it's only slightly) will get your pulse racing (and the pulses of everyone around you). Fabulously feminine, a silk blouse or dress will give you an ethereal air as you float around, dazzling the room.

The Push-Up Bra

It may be seen as cheating in some quarters, but a bra that gives you a bit of cleavage (whether it's on show or not) can make all the difference to your overall shape, line and silhouette, especially if you're wearing figure-hugging clothes. No need to go over the top if you've got small breasts, though – they often have their own appeal, *sans* bra.

The Colour Red

Red is the colour of arousal, of ripe strawberries, danger and lips. A red jacket or coat is a gorgeously bold statement that shows you're brimming with confidence, super sexy and ever-so-slightly hazardous. A red scarf is like a dash of tabasco, adding a touch of heat and spice. Red shoes hint at bedroom naughtiness; scarlet lipstick is the emblem of the *femme fatale*.

The Cashmere Sweater

When you're wearing cashmere, a touch from another person inevitably turns into a stroke: it's the ultimate in sensuousness. It's also miraculously warm to wear, which means that you don't need to bulk up like an overweight sheep when the temperature's low; you can be soft, svelte, comfortable and alluring. Perfect!

Sky High Heels

High-heeled shoes, like pencil skirts, restrict your gait and make walking a far more conscious activity. The higher they are, the smaller your feet appear and the more tottery you become, so they're not a million miles away from the notion of a temporary form of foot-binding, really. Is this why men love them, because we can't run away in them? Or do they get a kick out of feeling ever so slightly scared of being spiked by our heels? Either way, high-heeled shoes make your legs look longer and that's one great reason to wear them. Smart girls carry a pair of flatties in their bag, though – for the journey home (whether late at night or, ahem, early in the morning).

Boots

Find yourself a pair of nice-looking comfortable boots and everybody wins. You'll be snug and stylish and every guy you pass will look at your legs. What is it about boots that gets them going? Is it something to do with domination, some echo of army uniforms? Or is it simply the anticipation of unzipping or pulling them off? Either way, it works for us, because boots are often warm, practical and easy to wear, even when they're thigh-high with heels. Keep them on during sex and he'll love you forever.

The
Mating
Game

The Art of Flirting

> It isn't what I do, but how I do it. It isn't what I say, but how I say it, and how I look when I do it and say it.
>
> Mae West

Did you know that our first impressions of a new acquaintance are based mostly on appearance and body language, partly on voice and only minutely on what is actually said?

So, Ms Flirty Pants, just how good a tease are you? Can you get a discount at the shops by coquettishly raising an eyebrow? Does the postman knock twice to catch a glimpse of your smile? Can you get round your partner by putting your head to one side (like butter wouldn't melt) while gently stroking his arm?

Once you know how, it's easy to have the world eating out of your flirtatious palm. The simple truth is that we all want to be liked and flirting is about showing people you like them – male or female, young or old. You can flirt with absolutely *anybody*.

Primitive Flirting

Flirting is generally thought of as being sexually motivated and often (but definitely not always) it is. Scientists and psychologists love to extrapolate about how the art of flirting evolved as a social construct to ensure the survival of the species. It makes you wonder how it first originated. What sort of things did prehistoric man and woman say to one another?

He: *Uggg! I like the way you pick the nits out of your hair.*

She: *Why, thank you, kind Neanderthal! And I couldn't help being mightily impressed when I saw you club that woolly mammoth to death last week.*

Today, a thoroughly modern minx is a multi-media flirt, as adept with written as with spoken coquetry. Unfortunately, this means that she may be assailed by all manner of admiring trigger-finger mingers, especially at the office: 'Do U believe in luv at 1st site or do I have 2 walk by again?' should only receive a response if it's been transmitted with one hundred per cent irony.

OK, a text or email is a darn sight better than receiving a grunted compliment on your bearskin before being dragged into a damp cave by the hair ... but there's nothing like a good old-fashioned flirt: a little eye-to-eye contact and coy blushing, a touch of humorous banter and a bit of 'Come hither, Heathcliff'.

Feminine Intuition

The reason women are such natural flirts is not only because they're gorgeous, but also because they're adept at interpreting social behaviour and know how to respond appropriately. Men are apt to see things in black and white and think that anyone who is flirting with them is being sexual, whereas sometimes it's just a way of giving someone a compliment, or showing you like them.

> I'm just a natural flirt, but I don't see it in a sexual way. A lot of the time I'm like an over-excited puppy. I think I'm being friendly with someone and I'll sit in their lap. They think I'm flirting with them.
>
> *Kylie Minogue*

Older men are particularly susceptible and very simple to wind up. It can occasionally be nice to perk up an old codger by giving him a wink or a winning smile, but make sure he's safely out of reach. Eliciting an unwanted grope when you're trying to make someone's day can easily ruin yours.

In general, flirting is fun and should be practised at every opportunity. At the very least, it gives you a boost; at best it leads to romance and everlasting love. But let's not get ahead of ourselves, or we'll mess it up. Romantic flirting is something you do in the present, with the future hanging over you like a bunch of ripe cherries. Will you/won't you exchange numbers, chance a kiss, go home together and eat cherries? It could all go right or wrong at any moment, which is what makes it such a thrill.

How to Flirt

The best way to flirt is simply to be spontaneous. If there's a flirty vibe between you and your target, the rest often follows naturally. To upscale your coquetry skills, here are a few tips:

Tip 1. Looking directly into someone's eyes is such a powerful, emotionally loaded act of communication that we normally restrict it to very brief glances. Prolonged eye contact between two people indicates intense emotion, and is usually either an act of love or hostility – however, eye contact is the most common way to initiate a flirty exchange so it's important to get your timing right. Identify the guy (or girl) you want to flirt with and catch his eye; maintain eye contact for at least three seconds, then smile and look away. This will be just enough to get his blood racing.

Tip 2. If he starts checking the front of his shirt for spillage, or strides over and says, 'What are you staring at?' then you're probably getting a bit intense. Initial eye contact is often best accomplished out of the corner of your eye, with your body half turned away. Think sex kitten rather than tiger. He doesn't have know your true strength quite yet …

Tip 3. There's nothing like humour for breaking down barriers. If you're not feeling funny, take a quick look around the room and you're bound to find instant inspiration, because everyday life is funny. 'Whoops, the barmaid's false eyelashes just dropped into that man's pint of Guinness!' is enough to get the ball rolling. Laugh at his jokes (if they're funny) – it's an instant indication of compatibility and laughing releases feel-good endorphins. So it's a bit like getting high together.

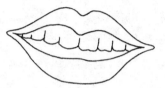

Tip 4. Feeling nervous? Asking questions is an excellent way of shifting the focus from you to him. Avoid clichés such as 'What do you do?' Instead, wrap up a little compliment in a question: 'You look happy! Did you just get promoted or something?'

Tip 5. Negativity is a real turn-off. If you complain about the world or your own problems, you might find yourself suddenly alone. So make light of your hatred of cold winter nights/your boss/the government if you really have to moan about them. Alternatively, give yourself a break and talk about things you *do* like.

Tip 6. A little risqué chat gets the hormones whizzing, so slip the odd light sexual innuendo into the conversation. Nothing clunky or forced, though, unless you preface it with, 'As my pervy old biology teacher used to say ...'

Body Talk

It isn't just the obvious bits that get men and women going – you need to utilize *everything* in your armoury if you want to get your flirting down to a fine art ...

Eyebrows

A raised eyebrow is also a crafty way of letting somebody know that you like him or her. But in Japan it can mean that you'd like to have sex with that person, so cock those brows with care!

Fiddling with your hair

You may not be able to stop yourself twirling a few strands, but be aware that most people know that it's a key element of female flirting. It's some latent monkey grooming instinct we've still got, apparently.

Fluttering your eyelashes

Don't be stupid. This isn't 1850s South Carolina.

Proximity

It's all well and good making eye contact across a crowded room, but you need to move close enough to strike up conversation. At four feet you are on the borderline between what is known as the 'social zone' and the 'personal zone'. Going too close may make you both feel uncomfortable, so keep a little distance, unless you are so magnetically drawn to each other that you just can't help yourselves.

Posture

Posture is a good indicator of whether somebody's interested in you. If a man likes you, he may stand taller or lean in towards you. You are likely to do the same, even cocking your head to one side – these are things we do subconsciously, which show the other person we are interested in him. If you like the other person, you might even find yourself mirroring his body posture – you can also do this consciously to make someone feel more at ease (see page 101 for more details on this).

Voice

Attraction is communicated much more by the tone of voice than by what is actually said. Depending on the tone, volume, speed and pitch, even a simple greeting like 'hello' can convey anything from, 'Wow, you're totally gorgeous – run away with me now!' to 'I find you totally uninteresting, your breath stinks, get me out of here, quick!' So think about how you sound when you start a conversation. You can practise this at home!

Smiling

Smile, smile, smile! Smiling is the ultimate seductive tool, unless you're a full-on dominatrix (in which case mainstream flirting might not be for you).

Touch

Once you're laughing, a touch on the arm can signal that you're comfortable with each other. But watch out, because it can seem a little bit icky. It's probably best to make sure it's a lighthearted push rather than a seductive brush, unless you're certain the game is going your way. Touching someone's hand is more intimate and you might want to save that for later …

Find a reason to whisper something in his ear

There's something very naughty about being up close to someone's ear lobe – just make sure you don't shout if he can't hear you the first time.

Mirroring

This can be fun and effective when you get it right. Mirroring someone's behaviour is basically imitating whatever gestures your partner is making. If he leans forward to share an intimate giggle, you lean in to meet him; if he looks at you meaningfully, you do the same.

A word of warning though: make sure you are not mimicking him. If he thinks you are it could really put him off. The best thing to do is to watch what he does, wait a few seconds then do the same.

Flirty Poses for When He's Talking

Pose 1. Lower your chin, turn your head a fraction to one side and slightly tilt it, and look up at him intently.

Pose 2. Smooth your hair back on one side of your head, while keeping unbroken eye contact.

Pose 3. Slightly open your mouth (you know, the way Keira Knightley always does) and gently run the middle finger of one hand back and forth across your lower lip. This 'accidentally' gives him a teasing view of your tongue and is a lot more subtle than licking your lips.

Pose 4. If he says something remotely intelligent, raise your eyebrows a centimetre, throw your head back and give him a softly penetrating look. (Keep a faint trace of a smile on your face, or he might get intimidated.)

Flirt Success Indicators

Measure how well your flirting is going down with these dead giveaways …

♡ Pupils enlarge

♡ Face flushes

♡ Heartbeat and breath quicken

♡ Palms sweat

♡ Eyes light up

♡ Lips become redder and fuller

> **"** I hope to start enjoying flirting again when I'm seventy, like my mother did. **"**
>
> *Felicity Kendal*

Quiz: **Are You a Natural Flirty Floozy?**

1. Someone you fancy is going to the same dinner party as you. What are you most worried about?

   A What you're going to talk about.

   B What you're going to wear.

   C That your best underwear is in the wash.

   D Whether he's going to notice you.

2. If a man you fancy walks in the room, do you:

   A Get your friend to introduce you and relay a potted history of your achievements.

   B Try to catch his eye.

   C Bump into him 'accidentally'.

   D Ignore him.

3. The man you like is looking at you. Do you:

   A Make eye contact for as long as it takes to fathom his personality through the windows of his soul, and vice versa.

   B Make eye contact for two to three seconds, then smile and look away.

   C Lock eyes with him until he looks away.

   D Look away in case he thinks you fancy him.

4. Someone you like makes a suggestive comment. Do you:

   A Say, 'Be careful – one day you might have to make good on your innuendoes.'

   B Give him a coquettish look and say, 'Do you really mean that?'

   C Say, 'Walk the walk, don't talk the talk, big boy!'

   D Ignore the comment and move quickly on to another topic.

5. The person you fancy says something you don't agree with. Do you:

   A Quote Groucho Marx and say, 'I cannot say that I do not disagree with you.'

   B Say you totally agree with him.

   C Tell him he is a fool, but a gorgeous fool.

   D Frown and tell him he's wrong.

6. You're sitting next to a man you like. Do you:

   A Cross your legs and face him.

   B Smile when he smiles.

   C Rub his leg under the table.

   D Make sure you're not too close.

7. It's time to go home after a party and you've been talking to the guy you fancy all night. Do you:

   A Give him your card and ask him to call you.

   B Ask him if he wants to share a taxi home.

   C Ask him back to your place.

   D Wait to see if he asks for your number.

8. When you're at a party, do you usually talk to:

   A Men and women.

   B Mostly men.

   C Only men.

   D Anybody who looks approachable.

9. You are out in a café and you notice someone checking you out. Do you:

   A Surreptitiously get out the literary novel in your bag with the cover facing his way.

   B Let him know you know he's checking you out with a knowing smile.

   C Smile and give him a little wave.

   D Give him the evil eye.

10. When you meet someone you like, are you:

   A More thoughtful.

   B More giggly.

   C More provocative.

   D More nervous.

11. If a guy tells you that you are beautiful, do you:
    A Say, 'Beauty is truth, so I'll assume you're being sincere.'
    B Say thank you and smile.
    C Tell him he's hot too.
    D Blush and look away.

Answers overleaf ...

Answers

Mostly As

You are flirtatious in an intelligent and provocative way, although sometimes you can be a bit of a clever clogs. Hey, remember – it's not all about you! You're not too forward and you're not too shy, yet maybe you lack sexual confidence, which is a shame, because you've got all the mental acuity to be an arch temptress.

Mostly Bs

You are the Queen of Flirts. You know all the classic moves and your body language is spot-on; you find it easy to attract a man and reel him in. You'll have no trouble getting the man of your dreams, unless he's looking for a quirkier gal. Occasionally, it might help to think outside the box, though ... just for fun!

Mostly Cs

You're hot to trot, but flirting's not your style. You'd rather cut to the chase and get it on. If you want to learn to flirt, try hanging back a bit and taking a more subtle approach. Less obvious body language and a softer verbal approach allows you more room to manipulate a social situation. (In other words, you might get what you want more often.)

Mostly Ds

You are a shy bird of paradise, which can be very appealing, but if you want to be more of a flirt, you should try to loosen up and stop being so scared. It's all there, but you're not sure how to use it. Try to be more confident and use your body language to indicate your interest. What have you got to lose? It's time to come out of your cage and enjoy life!

Dating with Attitude

In 1995, a couple of American women published a best-selling book called *The Rules*, which contained all kinds of strange, old-fashioned advice for single females, such as: don't offer to pay on a date; don't talk too much; end the date first. But what if a) you earn the same or more than he does and want a man who doesn't live in the Dark Ages; b) you are actually a very, very interesting conversationalist; and c) you want to get him back to your place?

For individual women looking for men who are looking for individuality in a woman, there's only one golden rule to follow on a date and that is: Break All The Rules. There's only one thing that's going to attract your perfect lover and that is YOU. So don't change yourself – there's nothing more disarming than the genuine article.

If you see someone you like, talk to him. If he's not interested or he bores you, walk away. If you like him, get his number or give him yours. If he doesn't call, so what? If he does, have a chat – make a date at a time and a place that suits you. Off you go!

Tip: Never obey the 'two-day rule' (which says that you should wait two days after meeting him or after your last date to phone him). If you want to call him, call him! Just don't pester him …

Useful Dating Advice

The best advice is to do what feels right – whether or not that fits in with 'accepted' dating etiquette. But you might find these suggestions handy before you leap out into the heady, and often confusing, world of dating.

♡ There's little point going on a date with a guy you don't fancy. Either there's a spark or there isn't, and if there isn't, it's not really a date. As good old Britney Spears said, 'I know right off the bat if I'm interested in someone, and I don't want them to waste their money on me and take me out to eat if I know I'm not interested in that person.' Cruel to be kind really is best.

♡ It's a good idea to dress down on a first date, since you'll be at your best if you feel comfortable, rather than trussed up and terrified that your shoulder straps/shoe heels are going to snap. Or, if you prefer to dress up, at least try not to go overboard by making it obvious you're angling for hot sex/a lifelong commitment, unless you want to make it obvious, of course. But do wear your very best underwear – even if he doesn't get to see it, you'll feel good in it.

♡ Have fun, your way. If he doesn't like your kind of fun, you don't want be with him, do you? If he does, bingo!

♡ Offer to pay your way. If he objects, that's fine. You can always pay next time. If he says, 'Just put away your purse and don't bother your pretty little head about the bill,' either wrestle him to the ground, get him in a headlock and tell him how hard you work for your salary, or if you're into the submissive thing go for it!

Not a Cheap Date

Cleopatra, Empress of Egypt – famous for bathing in ewe's milk and honey, wearing exotic make-up, rolling naked out of unfurled rugs and seducing both Julius Caesar and Marc Antony – once bet Marc Antony that she could spend ten million sesterces on one dinner. He accepted the bet. The next evening they ate a very ordinary meal, but when the second course appeared – a cup of strong vinegar – Cleo removed one of her priceless pearl earrings, dissolved it in the vinegar and drank it. Winner!

Dating With a Difference

Instead of playing it formal and conversing awkwardly between waiter interruptions at dinner, suggest one of the following alternatives for your date …

A dib-dab-date

On separate strips of paper, write down two different cocktails, the names of two bars or pubs, and the names of two cafés or restaurants in the vicinity of your starting point. Then fan out the strips of paper with the names of cocktails on them and tell him to pick one, with his eyes shut. Ditto with the bar strips and eating place strips. Next, draw for the second cocktail, the snack and the place to eat it.

Later, if you like him, add an extra lucky dip round, with two identical strips of paper that both say 'Kiss me' on them. Or if you're feeling especially naughty they can say, 'Back to mine?'

The freewheeler

Meet at a famous landmark – under a clock, in front of a statue or a building – and take it from there. No other advance plans allowed.

The blindfold

Meet him, blindfold him and lead him whither you want – though it's probably best to make sure he's game first, and bear in mind it might be rather tricky in a city centre …

IC/YC (Also known as I choose/you choose)

This one's simple: he chooses where to have a drink; you choose a place for a starter; he chooses somewhere else for a main course; you choose where to go for pudding, coffee and/or liqueurs. You can tell a lot by his choices – and give away what you want to with yours.

> Nothing defines humans better than their willingness to do irrational things in the pursuit of phenomenally unlikely payoffs. This is the principle behind lotteries, dating and religion.
>
> *Scott Adams*, cartoonist and author

Don't Forget to Have Fun

If you suddenly discover you're no longer having fun with the whole dating game, it's time to give yourself a good nudge and start enjoying yourself again. Here are a few tips to make sure you don't take it too seriously ...

♡ Take tiny flash cards along to any speed-dating session. Write something on each – anything from 'Whoops', 'Eek' or 'Yum' to swear words or 'The guy before you had really bad BO'. Subtly lift a card up, as the fancy takes you.

♡ When an undesirable comes along, decide which animal he most resembles and then ask his opinion of that animal: 'Are you a fan of guinea pigs?' Or say, 'I have one question and one question only for you: which is your favourite novel by Proust?' Ding! He won't tick your box or ask for your contact details. Get rid ...

♡ If you fancy him and there's a rapport, just follow your instinct when it comes to the question of sex. If it's right, it's right – even on the first date (make sure you use protection). Sleeping with him sooner rather than later is not going to change anything, unless he's only after one thing anyway, or is old-fashioned, chauvinistic or gay (i.e. probably not all that desirable, unless your preference is for sexist homosexuals with Victorian values).

> " Sex without love is an empty experience, but as empty experiences go, it's one of the best. "
> *Woody Allen*

♡ You don't have to play hard to get, but be cool if you know how. (If you don't know how to be cool, and if he's right for you, he'll love the fact that you're uncool.) Send him a sexy text message the day after, then turn the heat down a bit for a day or two. Nothing like a bit of withdrawal to make him want more. Tip: dump guys who quibble over text spellings.

♡ If you had fun in bed, text or email him a photo of a saucy part of your body that might appeal. This is known as 'sexting' and it's really good fun (make sure you get the lighting right, to avoid showing off pimples or cellulite). It's best to be certain you can trust the guy first, however, since you don't want to end up having your naked body shown round all his mates, or worse still, ending up on the internet.

♡ If it fizzles out or doesn't take off, don't fret. There's always another date out there. It's the law of averages. There are six billion people on the planet: three billion are men; maybe one billion are dateable age; perhaps you would only fancy a million of them; in your nearest city, there are probably several thousand hunks, even a hundred thousand if it's a big city; in other words, there are *loads* of fanciable men everywhere. Oh yes, plenty more fish in the sea.

♡ If he dumps you, he's obviously no fun. If he never rings, or isn't around enough, dump him. You can't be naughty with a reluctant man, and you can't play games with a man who always has to be the one holding the cards, so shrug him off and move on.

> 66 Don't cry for a man who's left you; the next one may fall for your smile. 99
>
> *Mae West*

Seductive Hints

At its best, seduction is a slow, sexy exchange between two people in the mood for sensuality. Alternatively, it's a chance for a woman to draw on thousands of years of subtle eroticism as she prepares to entice the man she wants into her boudoir. Here's how to let him know *exactly* what you're after ...

♡ Dress to impress ... yourself. If you're feeling sexy, you will be sexy. There's nothing like a flash of red lipstick to give a girl the glamour and confidence she needs to seduce.

♡ Whisper something to him; it doesn't matter what. His pulse will race at the warmth of your breath, the scent of your skin and perfume and the proximity of your lips as they almost brush his ear.

♡ Let something slip; feign a 'Whoops!' moment. Let your cardigan or vest-top strap fall off your shoulder, wait a beat or two, and adjust. Or make sure your skirt rides up your thigh an inch or so too high as you sit down or stand up – and smooth it back down again, as if hoping not to be seen.

♡ Stroke your lower lip with your little finger and look away dreamily as he orders a drink or a meal. When he turns back to you, let your hand drop from your mouth and give him a smile. He'll think you were having erotic thoughts. (Works even better if you *were* having erotic thoughts.)

♡ Show him your new earrings: pulling back your hair and revealing your neck can be very alluring.

♡ Mention your love of erotic art, from Rodin's nudes to Georgia O'Keeffe's suggestive blooms.

♡ Use words and phrases that evoke sensuality, such as 'excite' and 'turn-on', e.g. 'Travelling really excites me. Seeing new places turns me on.'

♡ Look at his lips and imagine kissing him. He'll sense it.

♡ Stretch like a cat at the end of a meal, or when you're leaving a bar. As you do so, put your hands behind your neck, put your head on one side, stick out your chest a little and arch your back. Sex will be on his mind as you leave.

Cooking for Pleasure

It is said that the way to a man's heart is through his stomach. But is this because men are greedy, or because the spur for sexual desire originates in the hypothalamus, the part of the brain that also governs our appetite for food and drink?

Irrepressible optimism is a key element of the naughty ethos, so let's go for the latter option and aim for his hypothalamus, via his luscious lips. No need to tell him what you're up to, simply serve up a seductive concoction of tried and tested aphrodisiacs – and reap the rewards later!

The Origins of Sex Food

> " Great food is like great sex.
> The more you have the more you want. "
> *Gael Greene*, US food critic

The hypothalamus connection is a relatively modern discovery, but the word 'aphrodisiac' derives from Aphrodite, the name of the Greek goddess of love, beauty and sexual rapture. According to legend, she cooked up love potions from herbs and roots in a mystical ritual involving music, dance and meditation.

The Ancient Greeks were not alone in recognizing the powerful aphrodisiac properties of the natural world. Almost all cultures have attributed sexual potency to certain foods and herbs.

Some aphrodisiacs gain their reputation from the principles of what's known as 'sympathetic magic', due to their shape and consistency. Asparagus springs to mind! The word for 'passion fruit' in Portuguese is *maracuja*, which is also a colloquial term for the female erogenous zone in Brazil. In Italy, this works for figs, known as *figis*.

Their rather erotic texture and comely shape make it easy to see why!

Other foods have properties that physically stimulate sexual arousal. Oysters, for example, are high in zinc, which is vital for healthy sperm production and erectile vitality. Perhaps this is why Casanova liked to slurp down fifty raw oysters before pouncing on his prey – but who can explain the slice of Roquefort he tended to follow them up with?

Incr–edibly Erotic Libido Liveners

It's almost time to get cooking! But first take a look at some of the many aphrodisiacs available to you ...

Asparagus

The seventeenth-century herbalist Nicholas Culpepper wrote that asparagus 'stirs up lust in man and woman' and this belief persists today. Scientifically it works, too: it contains potassium and vitamin A, which boost the sex drive, and is high in folic acid, which helps to trigger the histamines thought to be needed to reach orgasm.

Chocolate

The Aztecs drank a cocoa bean concoction called *xocolatl*, which they associated with Xochiquetzal, the Mayan goddess of fertility, and believed to be an aphrodisiac. One Aztec king declared that *xocolatl* was 'a gift of paradise'. Cocoa contains theobromine, caffeine and phenylethylamine, a clinically tested aphrodisiac.

Cardamom

Cardamom is a sensual spice. It cools the body when it's hot and warms it when it's cold. Top temptress Cleopatra loved to take cardamom baths. Say. No. More.

Ginger

The ancient Arabs, Greeks and Romans all agreed that ginger has a powerful aphrodisiac effect. The French seductress Madame du Barry famously gave it to all her lovers and even today it is used by men in the South Pacific to woo their women. A proven digestive aid that also increases the circulatory system, ginger heightens sensitivity in the erogenous zones, whether served pickled, sugared or raw.

Lobster

Lobster's aphrodisiac history can be traced back to the Ancient Greeks, who believed that Aphrodite was born of the sea and that all oceanic creatures were her playthings in the game of love. (Even crabs? Ouch!) Packed with the right kinds of nutrients for maintaining sexual desire, lobsters contain feel-good serotonin, Vitamin B-12, sulphur, calcium, iron and zinc.

Oysters

The first known reference to the aphrodisiac powers of oysters dates from the second century, when Roman satirist Juvenal described the wanton ways of women after ingesting wine and eating 'giant oysters'. Oysters' sexiness is in part due to their viscous texture, which conjures up all manner of erotic thoughts. They also happen to be very nutritious and high in protein.

Pine nuts

Zinc is an essential mineral for maintaining male potency and pine nuts are rich in it. They have been used to stimulate the libido since the Middle Ages.

Raspberries and strawberries

Often referred to in erotic literature as fruit nipples, these red, sometimes heart-shaped beauties should be hand fed to your lover.

Seaweed

In the Caribbean, everyone knows that seaweed makes you feel sexy. A combination of Irish moss (a mossy seaweed), milk, rum and spices is a still a popular aphrodisiac drink today. Seaweed contains vitamin B1, which combats tiredness, and B2, which aids hormone production. It is also rich in sperm–boosting vitamin E.

Sumptuous Seduction

So now you know which foods will get you both in the mood, put on your slinkiest dress, lower the lights, put on some mood music ... and present him with a bonk banquet.

Wet the palate

A drink before you eat can get your evening
off with a bang – well, if you make it champagne
it can! Add some strawberries and use a cocktail
stick to pick out the strawberries and then suck
gently on the tips before you crush them between
your teeth. Or you can try this potent cocktail ...

Aphrodite's love potion

Half fill a highball glass with ice and add the following:

A shot of brandy
5 fl oz pineapple juice
A dash of Angostura Bitters
A maraschino cherry (rich with innuendo)

Sensual starter

No fancy recipes needed here. Just serve up six oysters and six grilled asparagus spears each – and eat them alternately. You have to use your fingers and there are plenty of sensuous sound effects involved with both the oysters and the asparagus (lots of slurping and sucking) it's a mouth-watering way to begin your meal.

If this feels too obvious, try fresh artichokes instead. (Cut off the stems, and boil for ten to fifteen minutes, depending on the size.) There's a lot of sensuous fun to be had from ripping off the leaves, one by one, dipping them in butter and sucking them ... then cutting through the hairy bit to reach the fleshy artichoke heart. What's more, in days of old, artichokes were often prescribed to men wanting to improve their sexual performance ...

Steamy main course

You can't get a sexier main course than seared scallops – they're soft, fleshy and contain nutrients that raise the hormone levels in men and women – with a fig and rocket salad dressed with truffle oil and yam chips.

Seared Scallops

Scallops (4–6 per person, depending on size)
Olive oil

Salad:
4 figs
Bag of wild rocket leaves
Parmesan shavings
1 tbsp truffle oil
1 tbsp Balsamic vinegar
2 yams

Grill or fry the scallops in olive oil for about three minutes on each side, or until the flesh turns white. Peel the figs, chop them up and add to a bowl of rocket leaves and parmesan shavings. Drizzle truffle oil and balsamic vinegar over the leaves. Peel the yams and parboil them for five minutes.

Chop and fry the yams in a large frying pan, or baste them in butter and roast them in the oven for twenty minutes, or until golden brown. And serve to a *very* satisfied customer.

Orgastic Dessert

Chocolate and nutmeg truffle cake

180g of 100% solid cocoa or 70% dark chocolate
400 fl oz double cream
125g raw cane sugar
A large pinch nutmeg
A shot of rum
Optional cranberries to serve

Melt the cocoa or chocolate in a bain marie (a glass bowl over hot water). Whip up the cream and sugar until the mixture has doubled in size. Add the chocolate, nutmeg and rum to the cream and sugar mixture. Pour into a cake tin or dish and refrigerate.

As an optional extra you can serve with cranberries – they're packed with vitamin C, which boosts the sex glands. Voilà … Yes! Yes! Yes!

Somewhere for the Weekend

Naughty girls need holidays and weekends away to top up their levels of mischief. But where can you have the best fun? Here's a guide to some of the sauciest hotspots to escape to when you need that extra bit of va-va-voom.

Sexy City Breaks

Paris when it sizzles

Ooh-la-la! If it's passion you're seeking, then Paris is the city for you, the home of the Moulin Rouge, the Folies Bergère, and every other folly you can think of. It was here that artists and philosophers came in the nineteenth century to lounge around drinking absinthe until they were blind and visit brothels with the likes of Degas and Toulouse-Lautrec.

In the twentieth century, Henry Miller chose Paris as a backdrop to some of his more explicit novels, including *Under the Roofs of Paris*. The city was a constant breeding ground for new ideas and sensual expression.

Today, Paris is just as full of naughty creativity as ever. The food, the wine and the language all speak of seduction. The racy highlights of modern Paris cover a multitude of sins, including a 'fetish soirée' in a château on the outskirts, Madame Flo's burlesque show at La Mécanique Ondulatoire, a costume party at the Experimental Cocktail Club and any number of live sex shows.

Ich bin ein Berliner, baby

Berlin was the capital of the Prussian and the German Empire until World War I. It was a prosperous city with much to offer, but as The Depression hit in the 1930s, it slid into an era of debauched depravity. Smokey taverns were peopled with rouged, morbidly made-up characters, and the languid drawl of the legendary Marlene Dietrich could be heard from every corner.

After the war, naughtiness was replaced by outright nastiness, but today Berlin is back on form, living up to its hedonistic past in every way. Bohemian cafés and nightclubs have sprung up all over the city and it's one of Europe's creative hotspots, with artists flocking to experience its vibrant, edgy atmosphere. Poetry and electronica, street sculpture and high art, sex and sensuality – Berlin is a partygoer's heaven.

Flying down to Rio

Boasting two of the world's most famous beaches and crowned by Sugarloaf Mountain, Rio de Janeiro is without doubt one of the sexiest sun-soaked cities on the planet. Bronzed babes cruise the beaches in eensy-weensy bikinis; men parade about the shops in skimpy briefs; ladyboys lounge around, keeping you guessing: this is a city with such a seductive force you may never want to leave.

Wrecked in Reykjavik

Reykjavik is the nightlife capital of the north. Icelandic clubbers often don't go out until midnight and stay up through the night, especially in the summer, when there is only half an hour of darkness. After all, if there's no night, why bother with sleep?

In winter, head to one of the city's bars made entirely of ice. It's so cold the drinks are kept in the fridge to stop them freezing. If you're still standing after a couple of shots of throat-burning Icelandic schnapps, you may want to unwind naked in a hot geo-thermal spa, the perfect antidote to a wild northern night out.

Viva Las Vegas

Casinos, fantasy theme parks, cocktails, a mini Venice, blackjack, roulette, showgirls, pirate ships, marauding circus animals – Las Vegas is the sin city of the world, built for fun and frolics, and it's a great place for a totally mad hen weekend. Just don't take all your savings – and remember, what happens in Vegas …

Bangkok nights

Anything goes in Bangkok, especially if it's done with a sense of *sanuk*, the Thai word for fun. It's a great place for people-watching, from ladyboys to the Thai girls whose technique for shooting ping-pong balls at gawpers is highly unusual. There's a thriving travellers' social scene, offering an endless round of hotel and nightclub parties; the markets are legendary, the food amazing and the general ambience hot and steamy.

Wonderful, wonderful Copenhagen

Saucy postcards originated in Hans Christian Andersen's home town, which was once called the 'Naughty North' because of its bawdy bordellos and drunken sailors. Copenhagen started life as a Viking fishing village and there is still an elemental, untamed quality to the city, which today boasts a hundred lager microbreweries. Nightlife there changes fast and starts late, with clubs boasting an international line-up of Europe's best DJs.

Brighton rocks

Traditionally the home of the dirty weekend, Brighton was where George IV, the Prince Regent, built a palace to entertain his mistresses. Years ago, people seeking a divorce would spend a weekend with their lover in Brighton, make sure they were seen, and begin divorce proceedings by citing adultery.

Today Brighton is the gay capital of England and a hotspot for couples and groups of all sexual leanings. Whatever your inclinations are, what could be better than a big double bedroom in one of those grand seafront hotels overlooking the beach?

Largin' it in Ibiza

The third largest Balearic island's hedonistic heritage stretches back for thirty years and it has been nicknamed the 'Gomorrah of the Med'; you can party for days and nights on end – weeks even – without stopping, taking in as many disco sunrises as you like. The house, trance, techno and electronic season starts in June with Space and DC10's opening nights, but you can chill out and take in the Balearic Beat at Café del Mar all year round.

Baring All on the Beach

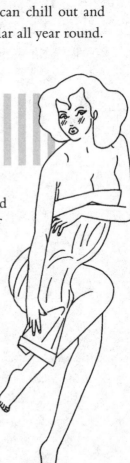

It's a real thrill walking, swimming and sunbathing naked … Here are some of the best beaches to go to strip off and feel the elements on your skin:

♡ **Haulover Beach Park**, Miami Beach, Florida attracts over a million visitors a year.

♡ **The Hawksbill Hotel Nude Beach** in Antigua is a tropical naturist paradise.

♡ **Studland Beach** in Dorset offers fine sand (that won't get in your knickers), sand dunes and a nature reserve. It's owned by the National Trust!

♡ There's five miles of sand and an abundance of wildlife at Canada's biggest nudist centre, **Wreck Beach**, in Vancouver.

♡ **Slapton Beach** in Devon is one of the UK's top naturist hangouts.

♡ Turquoise waters and golden sand characterize the beautiful **Panormos Beach** in Mykonos.

♡ Hidden from public gaze by steep cliffs, **Black's Beach** in San Diego, California is a firm favourite with West Coast nudies.

Strictly Bedroom

Pillow Talk

Information to Impress your Lover in the Bedroom

No, not like that – it's safe to assume you already do, you minx – but by astounding him with your knowledge of sex facts. You can arouse a lot more than interest with three simple words: 'Did you know …?'

Chinese whispers

The Chinese scribes believed sexual energy (*ching*) flooded the body with positive vital energy (*ch'i*). Women were thought to have an unlimited supply of *yin* energy, while men had only a limited supply of *yang* energy. (It's so true: we can continue to reach dizzying heights all night long but, oh dear, they can't.)

Men were not allowed to use up their *yang* essence without replacing it with *yin* essence. To do this, they had to delay ejaculation, making sure a woman had several orgasms first, thereby absorbing her *yin* essence. And if he didn't get enough *yin* essence, he was in danger of falling ill or dying. Full marks to the nymphet who thought that one up.

In the Tao dynasty, men and women believed they exchanged *ching* (sexual energy) during sex. New lovers were said to be full of *ching* energy. So the more lovers you had, the more energy you stored up. Orgies all round!

Indian inspiration

Kama Sutra, the original *Joy of Sex*, is an ancient Indian lovemaking manual written in Sanskrit in the second century. Actually, *kama* means sensual or sexual pleasure and *sutra* are the fundamentals of yoga, so *Kama Sutra* is more of a keep-fit spiritual sex guide. Famously, *Kama Sutra* describes every imaginable sexual position, from the 'Milk and Water Embrace' (best performed on an armless chair) to the 'Lotus' (good for hitting the G-spot), along with advice on smacking, moaning and oral sex.

There's lots of surprising stuff about kissing, too. A 'demonstrative kiss' is when a man kisses a woman's finger and her toe at the same time, for instance – as opposed to snogging her in front of all his mates from football. The female equivalent is when she kisses his thigh while washing his body – rather than tonguing him in front of his mother. Strange, huh?

Appassionata

Renaissance princess Isabella de Medici was the Barry White of her era. Isabella introduced erotic music to the sixteenth-century Florentine court, writing and singing madrigals about unquenchable love. The rhythm of her music was designed to mimic the act of love: caressing, exciting and pulsating, finally reaching an explosive crescendo. It definitely excited the aristos of Rome and Florence, but perhaps Isabella was a little too sensuous for her own good.

Her husband murdered her for being unfaithful by stringing her up in her bedroom in the Poggio Imperiale mansion in Florence, which she is still said to haunt today.

Japanese tease

Tie me up, tie me down, tie my bottom up! *Kinbaku*, which means 'beautiful bondage', is the Japanese art of tying up your bottom and other parts of the body in a visually aesthetic way. Evolved from a Samurai military restraint technique called *Hojojutsu*, it dates back to the seventeenth-century Edo period and is a precise art form using seven metres of hemp, jute or linen. The pressure of the ropes is particularly pleasurable when it squeezes the buttocks, breasts or genitals, apparently.

Far gentler than Western bondage, *Kinbaku* is taught by *sensei* all over the world, so it shouldn't be too difficult to find a teacher locally. Just don't mention it to your dad when he asks if you're doing any evening classes this year.

Europe's sexual history

Today the prevailing view of the gender gap is that men have a restless urge to sleep with as many glamour models as they can, while women want to settle down and be monogamous. But it was quite the reverse in the Middle Ages, when women were thought to be much more lustful than men, often insatiable. The model was probably good old Eve, who couldn't resist a fat bit of serpent in the Garden of Eden.

Women were carnal and men were rational, according to passages in Giovanni Boccaccio's famous 1350s collection of stories *The Decameron*: 'Whereas a single cock will serve for ten hens, ten men will struggle to satisfy ten women.' But was this just an excuse to encase women in chastity belts and lock them in a tower while the men went off to fight in the Crusades?

Sex statistics

♡ The British have sex ninety-two times a year on average, compared with 120 times for the French. But forty per cent of Brits are satisfied with their sex lives, compared with only twenty-five per cent of French people (although a recent survey concluded that seventy-nine per cent of Britons would rather have a good night's sleep than a night of passion).

♡ New Zealanders are level with Brits at a forty per cent rate of sex satisfaction, while a whopping seventy-three per cent of Indians are content in this area. Mumbai, here we come! Japan ranks the lowest, with only one in ten people happy with their sex life.

♡ Twenty-eight per cent of British women have poached their partners from other women and a third of British men have lured their partner out of another long-term relationship.

♡ Britons are likely to spend sixteen minutes having sex, compared to a worldwide average of eighteen minutes. Nevertheless, fifty-three per cent claim to have an orgasm every time. Who'd have thought it?

Erogenous Zones

Geographical Hotspots: the Body's Sensual Landscape

The term 'erogenous zone' was invented by psychologists in the nineteenth century as a way of describing parts of the body that have a heightened sensibility and stimulate sexual desire. Soon afterwards, anthropologists began to notice that different cultures eroticized different parts of the body – Asian men were said to love the nape of the neck, while Europeans apparently went wild for a wispy waistline; the Polynesians lusted after the thighs and the Chinese prized the feet; while Africans and Polynesians tattooed desirable parts of the body to give them an extra erotic appeal.

Fetish – Fact or Fiction?

In the 1930s, a psychoanalyst, J.C. Fugel, undertook the first study into the effects that clothes have on our view of the body. He concluded that men find bare flesh boring, but get excited when a woman accentuates or hides the erotic parts of her body. But was he just expressing his own preferences wrapped up in psychobabble? And did anyone actually get to see Fugel's bugle?

Fetishes have changed along with fashions. In the nineteenth century, when women wore long skirts and petticoats, the flash of an ankle was enough to get a rise out of a man. The 1920s flapper style accentuated the alluring beauty of the back; lips were emphasized in the 1930s; shoulders were big in the 1940s and by the 1950s attention had shifted to the breasts and hips; in the 1960s, the focus was on the legs. As the vogue spread for scantier clothes during the twentieth century, there was more room to display flesh and less room for the imagination. The body's erogenous zones withdrew behind increasingly small cover-ups, itsy-bitsy teeny-weeny yellow polka dot bikinis and thongs, for instance.

> " The mammary fixation is the most infantile, and the most American, of the sex fetishes. "
>
> *Molly Haskell*, film critic

So is it true that the more we bare and make them stare, the less mystique our bodies have? Not necessarily: the naked body is natural and beautiful, so it will always have its appeal. However, almost no one can resist stolen glimpses of forbidden flesh – whether male or female – because one of the roots of desire is curiosity. Never underestimate the lure of the unseen and the unknown … or the power of the sexual imagination.

A Sensory Guide to the Body's Erogenous Zones

Heady heights

The scalp has lots of nerve endings, so a gentle pull of the hair releases feel-good endorphins into the system. (No yanking!)

Amorous arms

Heaven is … a sensuous stroke that begins on the underside of your forearm, moves up the inside of your arm and then brushes down the side of your breast. Eek, take me to the bedroom now!

Sensual stomach

A barely there sweep of the fingers from hipbone to hipbone is totally amazing. Shiver my timbers – works every time.

Feeling feet

Feet are packed with thrillingly sensitive nerve endings. Press between the toes and lightly brush the soles of the feet. Then suck each toe, one by one. Try this with fingers, too.

Bringing sexy back

A back massage is a wonderfully innocent route to foreplay. For extra shivers, get him to run his tongue all the way down your spine.

Bawdy bottom

The gluteus maximus, or buttocks, are full of nerve endings. Rubbing or lightly smacking them will get those delicious endorphins racing. Make sure you hit the magic spot!

Naughty neck

Hot breath on the neck, the faint trace of fingers or a soft tongue can all be crazy-making in the boudoir.

Luscious legs

A lingering kiss to the ankle, the back of the knee and the inner thigh is guaranteed to kick up a storm of hormones.

Erotic ears

A playful nip on the earlobe is subtly suggestive. An exploratory tongue can be deeply sexy too (but only during the height of passion). In both cases, the element of surprise works wonders. Hey, where did that come from?

The rosebud

The clitoris has over eight thousand sensory nerve endings. That's more nerve endings than any other part of the human body, male or female. Oh yes, yes, yes. Don't you think it's about time you started taking full advantage of this information? Like, right this instant?

The glorious G-spot

The Gräfenburg spot is a patch of ribbed tissue in the vaginal canal. If he hits it, you'll know it. If he doesn't, see 'rosebud' entry above.

Tit for Tat

Anne Boleyn held off the sexual advances of Henry VIII until he was in a state of such frothing desire that he promised to divorce his wife and make Anne his queen instead. Anne's strategy was to extract favours from Henry by allowing him to touch parts of her body, one by one, including her inner thigh and her breasts, without going all the way. Her poodle king had to split the Church of England from Rome and suffer excommunication by the Pope in order to marry Anne, who went on to give birth to Elizabeth I. Her victory was short-lived, however; Henry later accused her of adultery and chopped off her head.

The Pleasure Principle

For pure pleasure-seeking, you can't beat the Ancient Greeks and Romans, who pretty much invented orgies. Hedonism derives from the Greek word for 'delight' or 'pleasure' and the concept is that pleasure is the only thing that's good for you.

The Greek philosopher Epicurus taught that pleasure was good and pain was bad, especially in a moral sense, except when pain led to a greater pleasure. It's a good starting point for finding happiness, whether or not you're into S&M.

Dionysus, the Greek god of wine, was known as the 'Liberator', because the cult of Dionysus centred around freeing yourself with wine, madness or ecstasy. His Roman equivalent was the god Bacchus. Bacchanalian parties were a scream, with lots of orgiastic partying in the woods and free drinks all round, at least five times a month.

A Sex-Life Less Ordinary

Orgies have been based on the pleasure principle for the last two thousand years and show no sign of disappearing. These days, they're held very much behind closed doors and enjoyed by a minority, but if you choose to indulge, here are some guidelines …

What to wear?

Of course, this is pretty much down to you and what you feel comfortable with – and, if it's a private party, rather than one of the advertised public ones, the hosts may well suggest appropriate attire before the event.

These are some of the more standard get-ups:

♡ A spandex tube dress

♡ A saucy French maid's outfit

♡ A PVC pencil skirt and basque, accessorized with a whip

♡ A g-string, nipple tassles and some bunny ears

♡ A black basque, a bow tie, top hat, long black gloves, a tiny skirt and thigh boots

♡ A mask – just covering your eyes or full-face *Commedia dell'arte*-style

Sex party etiquette for newbies

Dos

♡ Greet your host or hostess if it's a private party.

♡ Ask before you touch.

♡ Say no politely.

♡ Watch as much as you want.

♡ Express your fantasies and make sure they have been understood.

♡ Be clear about what you want and don't want to happen.

♡ Say thank you and perhaps even send a thank-you note if it's a private affair ('Thanks for a hot night' will suffice!).

Don'ts

♡ If you're shocked, try not to show it.

♡ Don't laugh outright at anyone or anything.

♡ No photography!

♡ Don't expect to see anyone again outside the swinging environment.

I Spy With My Little Eye

Catherine de Medici was the most powerful female ruler of the Renaissance era. She developed a taste for voyeurism when she married Henri, Duke of Orléans, at the age of fourteen, and her father-in-law watched them lose their virginity together in the nuptial bed. Later, Henri cast Catherine aside for his mistress Diane de Poitiers, but she sneakily watched them having sex through a secret peephole in her floor.

Everyday Thrills

Special occasions aside, what's a girl to do if she fancies a frisson of pleasure on a Wednesday lunchtime? The following provide the perfect antidote to those daily, um, frustrations …

The washing machine

A favourite with bored Sixties housewives, this is as simple as setting your cottons on forty degrees. Wait for the spin cycle and either sit on the machine or lean against it. Wriggle and press; wriggle and press. This is multi-tasking at its most enjoyable. Time to put another wash on!

The motorbike/scooter

Why don't more women drive motorbikes? It's a brilliant way of ensuring that you arrive at your destination feeling warm and fuzzy. Fire up the engine and sit slightly forward, leaning into the handlebars, or sit up straight with your legs well apart, and let the engine do the rest. Have a safe journey!

The horse

Much-loved by posh pubescent girls and their dissatisfied mothers, horse riding is an unquestionably sexy pursuit, even if you use a saddle rather than riding bareback. It's physically and mentally exhilarating to mount a stallion and gallop across the countryside, all the while savouring the friction of jodphur on leather; riding a plodding mule up a mountainside can also produce a slow burn in just the

right place. A donkey race along the sands at Blackpool just might do the trick, but it's recommended that you draw the line at Shetland ponies. They just can't take the strain.

A piercing

A clitoral ring is just the thing for the girl who wants pleasure at the snap of her fingertips. (Wait, ow! It doesn't quite work like that.) After a sensitive piercer has done the work, all it takes is a twiddle or a flick to spark a leaping flame of desire – at home, at work, in the park, on the train, at the movies, in a restaurant, wherever you like. Great fun can be had with this in boring meetings or while you're waiting for your computer to boot up.

Vibrating pants

These have a small, perfectly positioned pocket for a tiny clitoral stimulator, allowing you discreet, spontaneous pleasure wherever you want, whenever you want. Knickerbocker glory! For an electrifying shift of rhythm, try wearing them to a club and making sure they're 'on' while you're dancing. Wear them out to dinner and shiver like champagne blancmange under the table, or saunter through the supermarket aisles with a big smile on your face.

Vibrators: How to Choose the One That's Best for You

For home-alone satisfaction or fun with your lover, there's a huge range of bedroom accessories out there to suit all needs.

The Rampant Rabbit

Probably the world's bestselling sex toy, immortalized by *Sex and the City*, its shaft hits the G-spot while the bunny ears stimulate the clitoris. Oh my goodness!

Clitoral stimulator

Some women find it much easier to reach clitoral orgasm than vaginal orgasm, so these are great for foreplay or to enhance the action during penetration. They come in all colours, shapes and sizes, including a vibrator that looks like a toothbrush, for precision aim, a tiny powerful 'fingertip tingler' for discreet action during sex and another that looks like lipstick, for handbag-handy everywhere-orgasms.

Glove vibrator

With a built-in buzz at every fingertip, this is great for pre-sex massages, or just to get you going when you're alone. So many parts of the female body are erogenous that you don't need to go straight for the obvious destination, although it's so tempting that you might not be able to stop yourself.

Cock ring

How will this enhance your pleasure? It keeps him harder longer. Say no more! Some cock rings come with an inbuilt clit buzzer, so that means you're doubly happy.

Double dildo

Not for beginners, this should actually be called a triple dildo, because it's a sensational his 'n' hers thrill-provider with the potential for penetration, G-spot and clitoral stimulation in one.

Glow-in-the-dark dildo

For a really close encounter, this is a sci-fi vibrator for the thoroughly modern chick! There's something quite phantasmagorically fantastic about the way this dildo lights the way to pleasure.

Waterproof vibrator

Fun in the bath, jacuzzi, swimming pool or sea!

Bum beads

These go you-know-where and you pull them out on the point of orgasm. (If Bridget Jones did it with Daniel, it can't be *that* naughty!)

Double vibrating ring

One ring goes round the penis, another goes round the testicles and there's a vibrating bullet attached to enhance clitoral gratification. Ooh-la-la!

Flights of Fantasy

We all have certain things, people or situations that turn us on, but when it comes to fantasies we don't always have the energy or burst of imagination to get us really going – particularly after a day of deflecting the attentions of Bob in IT. So here are some scenarios to get your creative juices flowing. You'll be steaming up the windows in no time.

How to Create Your Own Erotic Story

The cheeky plot

This one should be fun, so keep it short; keep it simple; make it racy!

1. Sketch out your characters

   His role:

   gardener

   builder

   fireman

   teacher/pupil

   businessman/PA

   lion tamer

   Your role:

   lady of the manor

   bored housewife

   nurse

   teacher/schoolgirl

   boss/PA

   nightclub dancer

2. Begin by writing a scenario around your character.
   You could be in the kitchen sipping a cheeky glass
   of rosé, watching the gardener dig up one of your
   herbaceous borders. (If it works for *Desperate
   Housewives* it can work for you …) The sun is
   beating down. You watch him strip off his shirt to
   reveal a muscular torso. Droplets of sweat slide
   down his chest as he labours away. You undo the
   top two buttons of your silk shirt and apply a layer
   of peach-scented gloss to your lips before inviting
   him inside for a cool refreshing drink.

3. Dialogue can add a bit of sauce; keep it snappy, though. 'This job must keep you fit,' she said, glancing at his ripped stomach. 'And you? How do you work out?' he asked, eyeing her boldly.

4. Let your imagination run wild in the sex scenes. Set the tone by using good old Anglo-Saxon terms for the genitals, or metaphors such as lovebox and passionfruit. 'Wet', 'slide', 'lick', 'slick', 'suck', 'thrust' and 'explore' should all be used freely. Avoid polite terminology and medical terms.

5. Add some tension to stall the action and build anticipation just before the characters let loose – an awkward phone call or a knock at the front door will do it. Remember, you can introduce new characters at any point in the story, or bring in minor characters that you've already sketched from the beginning, like the gardener's assistant, or a sexy new neighbour who's been sunning herself in a tiny bikini in the next-door garden.

6. After the main characters have reached total satisfaction end with a witty exchange. 'Shall I come again next week?' he asked, buttoning his shirt. 'Only if you're prepared to work every bit as hard on my garden as you did today,' she replied.

The serious plot

Unlike the 'cheeky plot' the sex here needs to be intense and dark – think Sebastian Faulks rather than Jilly Cooper.

1. Set the tone of the erotic action to come with descriptions of nature and environment: if it's going to be a long, lazy session, then tropical sunshine or monsoon rain might set the scene. If it's going to be wild and frenzied, a thunder storm could run parallel to the main plot. You could begin with a short suggestive paragraph, an erotic metaphor or simile, using evocative words such as 'whip' ('the wind rose and whipped the walls of the house'), 'lap' ('the tropical waters lapped softly against the shore') or 'swell' ('the sea was angry, the waves swollen and high'). Metaphors can be simple and obvious – think caves, cellars, mountains and skyscrapers – or more subtle and personal to you.

2. Avoid harsh-sounding words and opt for ones that roll off the tongue – 'undulating', 'mesmerize', 'succulent', 'feathery', 'sensuous' and 'ripple'.

3. Keep dialogue to a minimum and try to make it slightly oblique.

4. In-depth description of the physical sensations experienced are a must, and the longer you can draw it out the better.

5. Keep the ending open and mysterious – no jokey asides in this fantasy, ladies ...

Once the story is ready, slip into the appropriate clothing and read it out to the man you plan to seduce with it – or, better still, get him to act it out with you. Alternatively, you'll get so turned on just writing it that you won't be able to wait for him to come round. See section on sex toys (pages 157–9).

Sexy Books to Inspire You

The Lover by Margarite Duras
Set in 1930s Saigon, this is the erotic tale of the affair between a young French girl and a wealthy Chinese man.

Delta of Venus by **Anaïs Nin**

A string of sexual encounters narrated from a female point of view, this is a fascinating exploration of the author's 'language of the senses'.

Tropic of Cancer by **Henry Miller**

Banned in Britain for nearly thirty years, this is a fictionalized account of the author's adventures with prostitutes, pimps, painters and writers in Montparnasse.

Lady Chatterley's Lover by **D.H. Lawrence**

Originally called *Tenderness* and banned when it first came out because of its explicit sex scenes and use of four-letter words, this is a sensuous study of complex relationships and intensity of feeling.

Story of O by **Pauline Réage**

Graham Greene called this, 'A rare thing, a pornographic book well written and without a trace of obscenity', but it has also been criticized for its cruelty and explicit sado-masochism. Not for the faint-hearted!

Chéri by **Colette**

A fabulous fantasy, in which a forty-nine-year-old courtesan remains irresistible to her younger lover. A deeply sensual novel.

Fanny Hill, or Memoirs of a Woman of Pleasure
by John Cleland
Carnal adventures galore as innocent but pleasure-loving Fanny sinks into prostitution and then rises back to respectability. Written in 1748 (and very obviously by a man!), it is considered to be the first modern erotic novel.

Song of Solomon **(from The Bible)**
Some of the most sensual love songs and verses ever written.

The Intimate Adventures of a London Call Girl **by Belle de Jour**
Sharp and witty, but not necessarily erotic, this is just a good fun, shockingly explicit read, written with breezy panache.

Hot Sex: How to Do It **by Tracey Cox**
Answers all your questions!

Erotic Bondage Handbook **by Jay Wiseman**
More ideas! How to tie up your lover/main character, or get tied up yourself.

Answers to Questions You Never Dared Ask

Even in these liberal days, there are still some topics that we don't feel comfortable talking about – or perhaps we're too embarrassed to admit we don't know. Whether it's what kind of wax to ask for at the beauticians or (blush) how to go about having a threesome, this chapter gives you some of the answers to help you make up your mind.

Which Way to Wax?

While *Sex and the City* might have taught us all about the Brazilian, does anyone outside the beauty industry know what all the other options are? Firstly, for those of you who aren't won over by the idea of waxing, it definitely has its upsides – less hair-down-there tends to make oral sex a lot more inviting, as well as making things easier for men who don't really know their way around. So whether you DIY or head to the nearest salon when it comes to tidying down below, here are some of the most popular options:

Bikini-line: quick removal of pesky side-stragglers.

European: tops of thighs and bikini sides taken off, leaving a neat patch on the mound.

Triangle: the hair is shaped into an arrowhead pointing downwards to the sweetie treat.

Heart: a favourite for Valentine's Day, this leaves only a trimmed heart-shaped tuft that can be dyed pink.

Moustache: everything off the front, except a horizontal strip where the labia meet.

Brazilian: everything off, front and crack, apart from a thin 'landing strip' or 'Mohican', a narrow vertical strip just above the fu-fu.

Hollywood: removal of absolutely everything, everywhere, for the nudie look.

If you're still not won over, here are the alternatives:

Sugaring: using a sugar-based mix instead of wax may prove less painful, because it sticks only to the hair and not to the skin.

Hair-removal cream: although it's a bit messy and chemically extreme, this leaves skin smooth for several days.

Shaving: a battery-operated bikini trimmer offers a quick and painless way to remove the hair-down-there. Of course, it doesn't leave the skin completely smooth and re-growth is fast, but there's no pain or ingrowing hairs, either. A wet razor gets closer to the mark, but should be used cautiously, unless you're prepared to be out of action for a couple of days!

Plucking: tidy up a wax or shave with a regular pluck!

How Do You Have a Threesome?

There are at least three ways to have a threesome:

♡ With a couple

♡ With your partner and a busty blonde

♡ With two men

You can do it with acquaintances or friends, but for the sake of your friendships you should be absolutely sure the people you ask will be up for it – be prepared to laugh it off as a joke if they're not; or you can answer a 'liberal' couple's advertisement in one of the broadsheets.

First things first

Set the rules: agree your boundaries and what you are and are not willing to do. Know your limits. Then …

Be safe: ideally, you've all got a clean bill of sexual health, but in any case use condoms and be aware of the possibility of fluid transfer by hand, mouth or genitals.

♡ Don't overdo the Dutch courage, or you won't be very good and you won't remember a thing.

♡ Don't get jealous, get involved! If the other two are on a vibe, don't sulk, start stroking.

♡ Be generous: it's about sharing between the three of you. Enjoy yourself and relish the moment. Life is not a bed of threesomes, after all.

♡ Don't invite the busty blonde to stay the night. She is not part of your relationship.

♡ Reassure your boyfriend that you don't prefer women/another man to him. This kind of pleasure is just for fun and experimentation.

Et voilà, you have the perfect recipe for a *ménage à trois*!

Where are Good Places to Have Sex Outside the Bedroom?

This is simply a case of using your imagination, but if you're too embarrassed or you're not feeling particularly inventive, here are a few suggestions ...

♡ In a car, preferably not while it's moving.

♡ On a park bench after dark.

♡ On the sofa in front of a sexy film.

♡ On the edge of the kitchen table or kitchen counter (if you're lucky, it will be just the right height).

♡ In the office when everyone's gone home (check there's no CCTV, though!).

♡ In the woods (just don't watch *The Blair Witch Project* first ...).

♡ For extra buoyancy when trying different positions, head into the water – if you've got a private jacuzzi or swimming pool (how nice for you) that'll do the trick, or if you're near the coast, head into the sea (preferably somewhere tropical). Just don't do it in full view of other members of public ...

♡ In the shower, with lots of foamy soap.

How Do I Talk Dirty Without Sounding Stupid?

While we might wish we could spout filth with the same easy purr as Samantha Jones in *Sex and the City*, most of us become more than a little tongue-tied when we're in the act. The trick is not suddenly to try to come out with raunchy suggestions – if you're not an extrovert it will sound weird and forced. The best dirty-talk of all is the encouraging sort: 'Oh yes, [insert name – and please, make sure it's the correct one] that's it, that feels good'. Or ask him for encouragement: 'Is that good? Do you like that?' Telling him what to do: 'Touch me there/Shut your eyes/Fuck me, now!' – is a guaranteed turn-on, but make sure you use a 'Please do this now!' beguiling tone, not an 'Oh for God's sake, you're doing it wrong' voice. And if you're really stumped, you can't do better than to pose the question, 'So what would you like me to do to you tonight?' in a kittenish voice. It's saucy and generous all in one go.

Fictional Floozies

If you want some seriously naughty role models, don't limit your search to the real world, take a leaf out of the books that you'll find these ladies in …

Moll Flanders is the eponymous renegade heroine of Daniel Defoe's risqué seventeenth-century classic. Born in Newgate prison, a bad 'un from the word go, Moll develops an early passion for breaking the law, first by selling her body, then with her light fingers. She marries five times (once to her own brother) and is eventually transported to Virginia. Oh, but she's so much fun!

Emma Bovary is the irresistible heroine of Gustave Flaubert's famous novel *Madame Bovary*. Married to a dull doctor, she escapes provincial village life by embarking on several adulterous affairs. Check out the breathless horse-drawn carriage sex scene …

Medea as portrayed by Euripides is so furious when her husband Jason runs off with another woman that she kills her children, cooks them and serves them up at a banquet. Guess who gets first slice of the pie? Poor philandering Jason literally chokes on his dinner when she tells him about the special ingredients. Lawks, talk about cutting off your nose to spite your face!

Becky Sharp, the star of *Vanity Fair* by William Thackeray, is one of literature's most savagely ambitious and admirable heroines. Not in the least bit content with her lot in life as a governess, she uses all her female wiles to seduce men, deceive women and advance her place in the world. You hate her, but you can't help but love her at the same time.

Estella, the adoptive daughter of Miss Havisham in Charles Dickens' *Great Expectations*, is deliberately raised to be a pitiless girl who breaks men's hearts. She becomes a cold woman, spurning the love that Pip (the hero) feels for her. But, hey, there's a kind-of-happy ending!

Constance Chatterley is the heroine of D.H. Lawrence's novel *Lady Chatterley's Lover*, a work so explicitly sexual that the author was forced to publish it privately in Italy, in 1928, and it wasn't licensed to be published in England until 1960. Why? Because it contained the word 'fuck'! Constance seduces her working-class gamekeeper and has scandalously enjoyable sex with him. Go girl!

The Girls of St Trinian's are the posh and naughty schoolgirls in Ronald Searle's *St Trinian's* cartoons. They wreak mayhem in an upper-class British boarding school, drinking, smoking, gambling and killing each other with hockey sticks. Ah, the best days of our lives! These motley minxlets run riot, play pranks and flirt outrageously with every poor male that comes within pouncing distance.

The Marquise de Merteuil, in *Les Liaisons Dangereuses* by Pierre Choderlos de Laclos, persuades her equally wicked lover, the Vicomte de Valmont, to seduce her cousin's daughter, who is engaged to her former lover. She promises the Vicomte a night with her, but when the dastardly deed is done, she refuses to honour her side of the bargain and takes up with another lover. Ouch!

How Naughty are You?

So, dear reader, you've worked your way through this bible of misbehaviour, but have you learnt your mischievous from your misguided, your wild streak from your needs-to-be-sectioned car crash, your naughties from your no-nos? Take this quiz to find out how naughty you really are ...

1. **You're in a meeting at work. You reach into your bag for a pen and pull out a pair of knickers by mistake.**

   Do you:
   A Blush, stammer an apology and stuff them back into your bag.
   B Say, 'I can't believe my flatmate pulled that old trick on me again!'
   C Wink, pick them up with your little finger and saucily flick them back in your bag.
   D Say, 'They're not ripped, they're crotchless, if anyone is wondering.'
   E Say, 'Whoops! What are my spare shag knickers doing there?'

180

2. You leave a shop and realize you've got something in your bag that you didn't pay for.

Do you:

A Rush back to the shop and confess all, apologizing profusely.

B Go back and jokily tell the security guard he's not doing his job properly.

C Take it back and get a refund for it.

D Keep it.

E Keep it and give it away as a birthday/Christmas present, pretending you bought it.

3. **A boring acquaintance leaves a message
on your answerphone asking when you're
next free.**

Do you:

A Ring back and wearily go through your diary
to find a date.

B Say you've got time to meet for a coffee and
quick catch-up.

C Text her from a friend's phone to tell her
you're dead.

D Ignore the message.

E Call back and say you're busy for the next year.

4. **While cooking for a dinner party, you realize that one of the ingredients you're using is seriously out of date.**

Do you:
A Call one of your guests and ask them to come early via the supermarket.
B Improvise, using something else.
C Use it, but insist everyone drink vodka shots before and after the meal to ensure all stomach bugs are killed off.
D Cook the meal without using the ingredient, however vital.
E Chuck it in anyway and make sure you snack on something edible beforehand.

5. **You've got a mild sexually transmittable disease and you've just pulled.**

Do you:
A Tell him exactly what it is you have, using full medical terminology.
B Mention it and show him how to please you safely.
C Pretend coyly that you never, ever go the whole way on the first night.
D Tell him you've got your period.
E Say nothing, use a condom and have your fun.

6. **After what you consider to be a bit of harmless flirting, your friend's boyfriend comes on to you.**

Do you:

A   Go cold and freeze him out.

B   Apologize for misleading him and make it clear that your loyalty is with your friend.

C   Tell him about your fetish for sumo wrestlers.

D   Say, 'You've got the wrong idea, you stupid ass!'

E   Tell him not to be ridiculous: you'd flirt with a sea lion if it bought you a vodka and tonic.

7. **It's your first night in bed with your new man and he strips off to reveal pendulous man breasts.**

Do you:

A Pretend nothing's wrong and fake an orgasm to spare his feelings.

B Fake feeling ill and go home.

C Shut your eyes and pretend you're bisexual.

D Ask him crossly why he didn't warn you.

E Point, laugh and say, 'Get lost!'

8. **You get drunk at the office party and slag off a colleague to the wrong person.**

   Do you:
   A Try to backtrack desperately the following day.
   B Make it clear that you were drunk and doubtless saying things you shouldn't have.
   C Roll your eyes behind the annoying colleague's back the next time you're in the room with them both.
   D Say nothing. You meant it, after all.
   E Be extra nice to the annoying colleague when the other person is around.

9. Your hot date asks you to dress up in suspenders.

Do you:

A Say sorry, but you prefer bare thighs and big knickers.

B Mix saucy lace with sensual satin.

C Put on a basque, a mask and a wig as well.

D Dress up in dominatrix gear and whip him mercilessly.

E Surprise him with something that turns you on instead.

10. **A gorgeous guy asks you away for a long weekend, but you've already used up your holiday at work.**

Do you:

A Ask if you can join him on the Saturday, because you can't take Friday off.

B Explain the situation to your boss and plead for special dispensation.

C Throw a sickie on the Thursday so that you've time for pre-weekend waxing and manicures, etc.

D Say there's been a death in the family and take a week off.

E Tell your boss you know he or she is having an affair and blackmail them into giving you the time off.

Answers

Mostly As
You're nice and caring, but lacking in confidence. Pleasing other people all the time isn't the route to happiness, so try to lighten up and be a bit more flexible now and then. Don't be afraid to experiment.

Mostly Bs
You're pretty straight, with a hint of naughtiness. You're popular and you probably won't have much trouble snaring a man. If you want a more interesting life, though, try to be a little more original. Mixing things up adds spice and fun!

Mostly Cs
You're downright cheeky! You've got your own way of doing things and you're lovable and funny with it. You're not afraid of new experiences, but try not to take your naughty pursuits too far, or you may end up regretting it.

Mostly Ds
You're honest and open, but you tend to see life in black and white and you take everything literally. What happened to your sense of humour? Did it jump off a cliff because it couldn't bear your company?

Mostly Es

You certainly know how to please yourself; nothing's going to get in the way of your good times. Compassion isn't a strong point, though. Watch out though – your naughty side could easily get out of control and turn seriously evil!